PECOS WILDERNESS

S A N T A   F E
N A T I O N A L
F O R E S T

by

Southwest Natural and Cultural Heritage Association

in cooperation with

Patty Cohn
and the Staff of Santa Fe National Forest

Stephen G. Maurer, SNCHA, Series Editor

D0920986

Southwest Natural and Cultural Heritage Association
Albuquerque, NM

Illustrations copyright © 1990 by Mary Beath
Cover photograph:
Near Head of West Fork Rio Santa Barbara by Rodney Replogle
Cover design by Mary Beath

Printed on recycled paper

ISBN: 1-879343-01-0

C O N T E N T S

4

PREFACE

Welcome to the Pecos Wilderness, one of the most beautiful sections of the Sangre de Cristo range of northern New Mexico. Most of this 222,673-acre wilderness lies within Santa Fe National Forest but a portion of it extends into neighboring Carson National Forest. As with all wilderness areas, the Pecos is roadless; however, an extensive trail system is maintained by the Forest Service to provide access to the high country.

This visitors guide provides valuable information about the trails of the Pecos Wilderness. It is detailed in many ways but it will not take away that feeling of adventure for anyone planning a trip to the high country. More importantly, it will help the visitor have a safe, enjoyable trip.

A considerable amount of time and effort has gone into the preparation of this guide. Individuals both within and outside the Forest Service have made major contributions to gathering the information. Many thanks to all those involved, especially to Southwest Natural and Cultural Heritage Association who initiated the concept for this series of visitors guides and who served as the catalyst for the preparation of this guide.

Enjoy using this trail guide as you explore the Pecos Wilderness, and please help us maintain this wonderful resource for generations to come.

LARRY ROYBAL
District Ranger
Pecos Ranger District

ACKNOWLEDGMENT

Many thanks to the 1989 and 1990 wilderness ranger crews—Bob Skaggs, Eric Dean, David Patenaude, and Deb Kanter—for their outstanding help in updating the trail descriptions; and to Lynn Bjorklund who wrote the original descriptions.

Thanks also to Tom Dwyer, Tony Roybal, Brent Abel, Diane MacFarlane, and Carol Torrez; and the Española and Camino Real ranger districts for their support, advice, and assistance.

INTRODUCTION

HISTORY

Little archaeological or historical research has been conducted within the southern Sangre de Cristo range, which includes the Pecos Wilderness. Isolated artifacts dating back to the Paleo-Indian period (7,000–6,000 B.C.) have been found in and north of the wilderness. Most artifacts date to the late Archaic period (900 B.C.–400 A.D.). Items which date to the Basketmaker culture (250–600/700 A.D.) and to late Pueblo IV, Anasazi times (1400–1600 A.D.) have also been found.

None of the sites surveyed displays proof of long-term occupation. It is thought that use by indigenous people was seasonal and temporary: groups went into the mountains for hunting and gathering trips during the summer months and returned to the lower elevations in the winter. The presence of points, knives, and scrapers associated with hunting, and the absence of grinding implements (manos, metates) linked with agriculture support this belief. The high-mountain peaks may have served as shrines, particularly in later Pueblo times.

Historic occupation of what is now the Pecos Wilderness began with the colonization of New Mexico by Spain in 1598. During the next 200 years, Spanish settlements pushed into the fertile river valleys of the Sangre de Cristos along the western flank of the mountains. The people from these villages (Cordova, Truchas, Trampas, Valdez, etc.) made periodic excursions into the Pecos for hunting, gathering, or grazing. Like the prehistoric uses, these too were of a transitory nature, leaving no permanent marks on the land.

Historic uses of the upper Pecos River area occurred primarily during the summer season when high-mountain meadows provided forage for livestock. Grazing may have begun in this area as early as 1825; cabin and ranch sites in the Cowles, Beattys Flats, and Mora Flats areas indicate increased grazing use during the later 19th and early 20th centuries. Grazing continues today.

New Mexico was annexed to the United States following the Mexican War of 1846. In 1873-75 the Wheeler survey party climbed and surveyed the peaks in the Pecos. Mineral prospecting began about the same time; George Beatty was an early prospector who built a cabin at the junction of the Pecos River and the Rito del Padre. Beattys Flats is named after him. This cabin and others in the wilderness built by early settlers no longer exist. Other prospectors also criss-crossed the area but only one mine of importance resulted: the Pecos copper mine located at Terrero. It was constructed in the early 1880s and was worked intermittently for over 40 years but did not become productive until the American Metal Company assumed control in 1929. Gold and silver were also extracted from the mine, which closed in 1939.

In 1892 President Harrison proclaimed the upper Pecos watershed a timberland reserve for watershed protection. No provision was made for administration, management, and use. The area was set aside and withdrawn from every use including logging, grazing, and mining. It was completely closed to the public. This area later became the Pecos National Forest and was later combined with the Jemez National Forest to form the Santa Fe National Forest. The Pecos Primitive Area of 133,640 acres was established by the Chief of the Forest Service in 1933. It was declared a Forest Service wilderness in 1955 and became part of the National Wilderness Preservation System on September 3, 1964, when President Johnson signed the Wilderness Act. In 1980 the New Mexico Wilderness Act added 55,000 acres to include more lands with wilderness character. The wilderness now totals 223,667 acres.

NATURAL HISTORY

Topography
The Pecos Wilderness is a heavily forested, high-elevation, and rugged mountain land, ranging from 8,400 feet to over 13,000 feet. Truchas Peak, at 13,103 feet, is the second highest point in New Mexico and dominates the landscape. Long, broad mesas are separated by river valleys. The Sangre de Cristo Mountains run northeast to southwest across the wilderness, separating broad mesas to the east from rugged canyons and ridges to the west. This wide variation causes many steep slopes and cliffs. Small lakes and perennial streams furnish water. The mesas and mountaintops give the traveler outstanding views of the surrounding country.

Geology
The Pecos is geologically diverse. Precambrian granites form the canyons and hills in the western section; Pennsylvanian sediments are found in the central Pecos; and Precambrian schists and quartzites are found in the eastern mountains.

In Precambrian times, seas covering the Pecos region deposited sediments which were compacted to form sandstone, shale, and siltstone. Surface volcanic flows and igneous granite intrusions mixed with these sediments. These rocks were compressed and uplifted into tightly compressed folds of east-west mountain ranges. These powerful forces metamorphosed the rock into quartzite, mica, schist, and phyllite. Over the course of hundreds of millions of years, these mountains were eroded into hills.

About 300 million years ago, seas advanced and covered the metamorphosed and igneous Precambrian rocks. The highest peaks, including

Truchas, Pecos Baldy, and Chimayosos, and the canyon headwalls of the Pecos, Valdez, and Mora rivers, were islands in this sea. The seas retreated and advanced several times, depositing layers of sandstone and limestone sediments over a period of 100 million years.

The Rocky Mountains began to be formed 70 million years ago and are quite young, geologically speaking. They were formed by mighty crustal disturbances concentrated on lines of weakness in the earth's crust which took place over millions of years. Since the Rockies were uplifted, the area has never again been submerged. The Sangre de Cristo Mountains, which run northeast-southwest across the wilderness, are the southernmost end of the Rockies.

Weathering and erosion stripped away surface rock and reduced mountain elevations. The ancient Precambrian granites were exposed and uplifted to form the peaks of the Pecos. The rivers cut through and exposed the Pennsylvanian sedimentary and Precambrian rock layers. Extensive glaciation took place 12,000 years ago. There were many small valley glaciers which sculpted and shaped the mountains, valleys, and hills. The processes of uplift and erosion are still occurring today, continuing to shape the landscape of the Pecos Wilderness.

Plant Life
The forests in the Pecos are primarily of pure Engelmann spruce at the higher elevations, mixed with some aspen, corkbark fir, and blue spruce. Ponderosa pine, Douglas fir, white fir, limber pine, bristlecone pine, and aspen are found at lower elevations. Large meadows are intermingled with the forests. Of special interest are the many diverse riparian settings found within the wilderness. Summer brings flowers to the mesas and forests of the Pecos. Indian paintbrush, iris, monkshood, thistle, false hellebore, gilia, lupine, monkeyflower, penstemon, columbine, yarrow, aster, and gentian are among the flowers that offer a bright show. Best times for viewing are June and July. Fall brings changing colors to the aspen and oak. Red, yellow, and orange leaves contrast with the evergreens and snowcapped peaks. Most of the trails in the wilderness give outstanding views of fall colors and wildflowers. Please leave flowers, leaves, and plants, living and dead, in the wilderness. They are important parts of the ecosystem, providing food, shelter, and soil nutrients.

Animal Life
The Pecos Wilderness is home to many mammal, bird, and fish species. These include turkey, grouse, raven, jay, junco, hawk, owl, pika, black bear, mule deer, elk, marmot, squirrel, chipmunk, weasel, snakes, and several kinds of trout. Ptarmigan and bighorn sheep, once native to the area, were hunted to regional extinction but have been reintroduced and are doing well.

The Wilderness Act directs that "the earth and its community of life" be unrestrained by man. Even though much must still be learned about the interrelationship of wilderness ecosystems, one of the basic goals is to manage wildlife habitat in a manner which contributes to wilderness values. The Santa Fe National Forest manages wilderness use to maintain or enhance threatened and endangered species habitat, native plant and animal species, and allow the reintroduction of native species.

Climate
The high altitude of the Pecos provides a cool change from the lower deserts and brushlands. Temperatures vary with season and elevation. Summer daytime temperatures average 70° F, dropping to the high 30s at night. Fall and spring temperatures range from highs in the 50s to lows in the teens. Winter temperatures below 0° F are not uncommon. May and June are usually dry months. In July and August, however, showers and thunderstorms occur almost every afternoon. Lightning strikes above timberline pose a hazard to travelers. Winter storms can start as early as October and continue through April. Winter snowpack may lie on the land as late as June 15, stopping or slowing travel to and within the wilderness. Annual precipitation is from 35 to 40 inches. About half comes from summer rains and half from winter snows.

WILDERNESS USES

Domestic Livestock
Some people do not realize that the grazing of livestock is allowed in a designated wilderness. This grazing was provided for by Congress with the passage of the Wilderness Act of 1964. The Forest Service objective for livestock management in wilderness is utilization of the forage resource while maintaining wilderness values.

Structural range facilities, such as barbed wire and wooden fences, corrals, stock tanks, spring developments, etc., are also authorized. Congress has also provided for certain circumstances in which grazing permittees may utilize motorized equipment as well as motor vehicles inside wilderness areas. The Forest Service must analyze and approve all such requests on a case-by-case basis.

If you use corrals, please be sure they are not damaged. Also, do not deny cattle access to water by camping at inappropriate locations. Close all gates unless it is apparent they are meant to be left open.

Mineral Exploration
The Wilderness Act also authorizes mineral development and mining activities when warranted. All wilderness areas were closed to mineral entry at midnight, December 31, 1983. No new claims can be staked in any wilderness. Working a valid claim may be permitted, but it must be

conducted in a manner that is as compatible as possible with preservation of the wilderness environment.

Hunting and Fishing

Hunting and fishing are allowed in the Pecos Wilderness. Wildlife is the property of the state of New Mexico and all applicable state hunting, fishing, and trapping regulations apply. Information on hunting and fishing regulations or seasons can be obtained from the New Mexico Department of Game and Fish, Villagra Building, Santa Fe, New Mexico 87501, or call (505) 827-7911.

Natural Fire Management

Fire has been a significant force in shaping the character of the Pecos Wilderness. Natural fire alters the composition of plant communities and renews the process of plant succession; provides diverse wildlife habitat and creates a desirable patchwork of vegetation; regulates the accumulation of natural fuels; accelerates soil nutrient cycles and energy flow; and affects forest insects, parasites, and pathogens.

Until recently fire was viewed only as a destructive force and its role as a natural element was overlooked. But our understanding of fire has improved over the last decade and fire is now recognized as a natural and desirable part of the wilderness ecosystem.

One of the biggest fires in the recorded history of the Pecos occurred in 1887 when a fire that had begun in Big Tesuque Canyon burned up the slopes of Lake Peak, Santa Fe Baldy, and Pecos Baldy, creating the bare slopes that are still visible. For two months the fire burned unchecked, crossing the Pecos north of Cowles and burning across the mountains north of Las Vegas toward Wagon Mound where it was finally checked by a crew cutting railroad ties.

The Pecos Wilderness Natural Fire Management Plan allows for natural fires to burn, provided desirable weather, fuel moisture, and fire behavior conditions are met. All fires are monitored by qualified personnel.

RULES AND REGULATIONS

Congress passed the Wilderness Act in 1964, establishing the National Wilderness Preservation System which today consists of 474 units totaling 91 million acres. These lands stand as living testimony to the wisdom and foresight of Congress and the American people for preserving wilderness for future generations.

The Wilderness Act sets aside huge tracts of land as areas "where the earth and its community of life are untrammeled by man, where man himself is a visitor who does not remain." The act mandates that wilderness areas be "administered for the use and enjoyment of the American people in such a manner as will leave them unimpaired for future use and enjoyment as wilderness." Accordingly, wilderness areas are protected from development—roads, dams, permanent structures, timber cutting—and, since 1984, from new mining claims and mineral leases. Wilderness is also closed to motorized equipment and mechanized transport such as cars, aircraft, hang gliders, motorcycles, bicycles, chain saws, and generators. Group size is limited to a maximum of 15 people or, in the case of horseback trips, the number of livestock is limited to 15. Length of stay is limited to 14 days. Permits are not required to visit the Pecos Wilderness except for any type of guiding or outfitting services which are not on a total cost-share basis.

Other restrictions established for the protection and management of the wilderness resource are:
• no shortcutting switchbacks on a forest trail;
• all camping equipment or personal property, including trash, must be removed when leaving the wilderness; camps and equipment may not be stored in the wilderness;
• camping is prohibited in all lake basins in the wilderness and along the Pecos River at Beattys Flats and Pecos Falls;
• no camping within 200 feet of water or a forest system trail.

Please check with the local ranger station to find out what other rules and regulations may be in effect at the time of your visit.

WILDERNESS PHILOSOPHY

Throughout America's history, people have seen the expansion of civilization as a threat to wilderness and have spoken out for preservation of the wild lands. To Henry David Thoreau, wilderness was a "tonic" for the human condition. To John Muir, wilderness represented "the hope of the world." Former Supreme Court Justice William O. Douglas felt that wilderness helped preserve man's "capacity for wonder—the power to feel, if not see, the miracles of life, beauty, and of harmony around us."

Wilderness holds special values for each person. To some, these wild lands represent an opportunity to reflect on the role of humankind as a part of the community of life rather than as a conqueror of nature. To others, wilderness provides a temporary escape from the pressures of a highly technological and demanding society, an escape from the "man-made" into the "natural." More importantly, wilderness is an attitude, a recognition that the community of life exists for its own sake. A wilderness designation provides an opportunity for life to continue evolving unaffected by human control. Just as wilderness provides humans a place to escape from modern civilization, the designation protects an area from human development. The value of wilderness to future generations will not come through designation alone, however. We must learn to properly care for the land which has been set aside as an "enduring resource of wilderness."

BACK-COUNTRY ETHICS

Because of the popularity of wilderness areas and their increased use, we are in danger of literally "loving them to death." Management seeks to reduce impacts recreational use, such as vegetation damage, litter, water pollution, erosion, and crowding. One way to achieve this is by practicing "low-impact camping." This is a non-regulatory type of management that does not directly restrict the freedom and spontaneity of wilderness users (as compared to regulatory types of management such as assigned campsites, quotas, and permit systems). These low-impact camping methods are intended to promote the least visual and physical impact when camping and to help preserve the wild character of the land.

A. Planning and Preparation

A well-planned trip will go a long way toward helping it be safe, enjoyable, and memorable.

- Plan to go at the least crowded time and to the least crowded area.
- Limit group size. Large groups have a greater impact on the land than small ones.
- *You are responsible* for knowing the rules and regulations of the area you are going to. Check with the ranger station if in doubt.
- Repack your food. Eliminate cans, bottles, and foil-lined products. Repackaging food in plastic bags gives you less weight to pack and less garbage to pack out.
- Do without heavy, unnecessary items such as a skillet, axe, and firearms. By carefully selecting food and equipment, no more than 40 pounds should be needed for a week-long summer trip.
- Don't forget a garbage bag to pack out wastes.
- Choose clothes, packs, and tents with earth colors such as green, brown, or blue. These colors blend in with the environment and reduce the visual impact on others.
- Be prepared for changing weather conditions. Take rain gear, a jacket, and a set of dry clothes.
- Miscellaneous small safety items are important: compass, flashlight, candle, first-aid kit, pocket knife, sun screen, waterproof matches, whistle, mirror, and nylon cord or wire for equipment repair.
- Leave your itinerary with a friend or relative. Try to follow the plan, at least as far as the return date is concerned.
- Become familiar with the area. Know where you are going and how you are going to get there. Study maps of the area and visualize the terrain. Expect weather changes and fewer daylight hours in fall and winter.

- Make sure you carry a compass and maps, and know how to use them. Trail signs are damaged by vandals and wildlife; do not rely on signs to find your location.
- Know your limits! Be realistic about how far you can hike when planning your route. Physical conditioning for a trip is extremely important. Don't assume anything. Take several practice hikes to condition the body before undertaking a back-country trip. Travel only as fast as the slowest person in the group.

B. Hiking on the Trail

Here's how to walk lightly on the land:

- When encountering horse or llama groups while hiking, give them the right of way. Step off the trail on the downhill side, stay quiet, and let the group pass. Horses can be easily spooked by hikers or sudden movements.
- If you are traveling with llamas, please move off the trail when approached by horses.
- Do not shortcut switchbacks. This causes erosion and vegetation and trail damage. Shortcutting also creates unsightly spur trails that can confuse hikers.
- Stay on designated trails. Trails are built to handle water drainage and provide a good, safe route for travel. Going off the trails causes vegetation damage and leads to erosion. If the trail is muddy, walk through the mud to avoid making the trail wider.
- Dogs disturb wildlife and other campers. If you must bring a dog, be sure it is kept under control *at all times*. Leashes are required in Santa Fe County.
- If hiking cross-country, try stepping on rocky or compacted soil and have group members scatter and follow different routes. This will avoid vegetation and soil damage.
- Do not leave trail markers (rocks, flagging, etc.). These may cause confusion to other hikers.
- Travel quietly so as not to disturb others. You'll see more wildlife too!
- Leave the flowers, plants, rocks, antlers, and any other natural objects in the wilderness. They are important parts of the environment, providing food and nutrients. Others will get a chance to enjoy them when you leave them behind. Take only pictures, leave only footprints.

C. Setting up Camp

Using low-impact camping methods will help protect the fragile, high-altitude areas of the Pecos.

- Select a campsite away from trails and other campers. Pick a tent site which is on level ground in a sandy or forested area with adequate drainage. Picking a spot in lush meadows or other areas may damage the site permanently. Do not trench your tent; it is unnecessary if you choose a site with good drainage.

- Water sources are abundant but they must be carefully protected from pollution. Camp at least 300 feet away from springs and streams.
- Try to have no more impact on the site than is necessary. We don't make log chairs or bough beds anymore. These things can make a campsite more like home but are not worth the damage to the environment.
- Naturalize your site when you leave: scatter leaves and twigs over your campsite; make it look like you weren't there.
- Cigarette butts, pull tabs, orange peels, apple cores, foil, etc. are all litter. PACK IT IN, PACK IT OUT! Litter on the trail or at the campsite can ruin someone else's trip. Even things that are biodegradable take a long time to decompose. For example: paper plates—3 months; tin cans—10–100 years; cigarette butts—25 years; plastics—300 years; aluminum/foil—forever; orange peels—2–5 years.
- Also, please pick up litter left by others; that's just plain nice of you!

D. Horse Travel

Some visitors use their own saddle and pack stock as a means of travel. Here are a few hints which will help to minimize the effects of stock use and help to make a safe trip.

- Keep the number of stock to a minimum! Leave the skillet, axe, firearm, and heavy canvas tent at home. The use of lightweight foods and equipment can reduce the number of animals needed.
- Make sure your stock is "trail wise" and used to mountain travel and to the high altitude. *Before the trip begins,* familiarize your stock with equipment you will use on the trip. This will help avoid accidents and injuries.
- Although grazing is allowed, it may be limited in some areas. Carry supplemental feed such as pellets and rolled grain. Processed feed saves water and vegetation and prevents introduction of plants foreign to the wilderness. Do not bring in hay, as it may contain seeds of noxious weeds and non-native species.
- Keep animals away from campsites and water sources except during watering time. This will minimize water pollution and damage to fragile riparian areas, and will decrease the number of flies at your campsite.
- Route planning must consider care and feeding of animals. Campsites must provide for the animals' needs for water, feed, and holding.
- Do not tie stock directly to trees, as this damages tree roots and compacts the soil at tree bases. If you must, tie them to trees larger than 4 inches in diameter and for only short periods of time, such as at a break. At camp, use a picket or hitchline to hold animals. Use tree-saver straps and move animals frequently to avoid soil and vegetation damage. Keep them away from the trail and other campsites; relocate

picket pins daily.

- Scatter manure and other debris resulting from animals standing in a particular area. Remove all ropes or other materials used to confine animals when camp is moved.
- Lead, do not drive, pack stock and do not allow any stock to cut switchbacks.
- Respect the rights of others when on the trail. Remember, hikers often do not realize they can easily spook livestock.

E. Fire

During certain times of the year, fire hazard can be extremely serious in the wilderness. We ask that you be especially careful.

- First, decide whether or not you *really* need a campfire. Firewood is scarce in high alpine areas and at popular camping spots. Dead and decaying wood provides habitats for living organisms and returns nutrients to the soil.
- Use a lightweight stove for all cooking whenever possible. It is quick and clean and works in all weather conditions. A stove makes excellent survival gear in cold, wet weather.
- If you need to build a fire, collect only wood that is dead and on the ground. Do not cut down dead trees, saw off dead branches, or cut down live trees and branches. Green wood will not burn and large branches and logs may be too large to burn completely. Use smaller sticks which burn completely and are best for cooking.
- If you need to build a fire, use one of these fire-building methods for the least impact on your campsite:
  1. Use an established fire ring if one is available. Don't make a new fire scar on the land if one already exists. Scatter the rocks and ashes and naturalize the site when you leave.
  2. Use the firepit method: remove sod or topsoil in several large chunks or dig a small pit, making sure duff (dead leaves and twigs) surrounding the area is cleared. Do not put a rock ring around the fire. After you are done make sure all coals are burned completely and out cold. Scatter the ashes, replace the sod, and spread the duff back over the area.
- Do not try to burn food wastes or paper with foil linings. Fires usually do not get hot enough to completely burn food wastes. Paper with foil lining will not burn at all. Pack these wastes out.
- When you're done with your fire, be sure that no trace is left. Pick out trash that did not burn. Naturalize the area: scatter the rocks, replace the soil, and spread duff back over it. Also scatter firewood that was not used. Remove logs or rocks used as seats. Black rocks and gray, ashy soil are ugly reminders of man's intrusion upon the wilderness.
- If you smoke, please be sure all matches, ashes, etc. are out cold be-

fore moving on. Pack out the cigarette butts and dead matches!
- Do not build a fire on a windy day; do not leave any fire unattended, including cooking fires!

F. Sanitation

Serious disease problems have been traced to poor personal hygiene and food-handling practices. Giardia or "backpackers' disease" is the most common affliction resulting from poor sanitation.

- When nature calls, select a suitable spot at least 300 feet away from any water source, including dry springs and creeks. Dig a hole 4 to 6 inches deep. After use, fill in the hole completely, burying waste and toilet paper. Do not burn paper; it does not burn completely and may cause a fire. Bury waste left by your dog also.
- A small garden trowel and a roll of toilet paper, all in a small ditty bag, make a fine personal toilet.
- Large groups should establish a latrine or use a portable toilet for packing out waste.
- Do not wash dishes, clothes, or yourself in any water source. Even biodegradable soap pollutes water, making it unsafe for humans and animals to drink. Carry water back to your campsite and wash there. Throw dirty water onto rocks or bare ground.

G. Safety

As in other types of outdoor activity, back-country travel poses some potential problems and hazards.

- WATER—Unfortunately, it is no longer safe to assume that clear, cool water is okay to drink. Giardia, an intestinal parasite also known as "backpackers' disease," is infecting back-country water sources. Although many of the springs and creeks in the wilderness run year-round, all water should be considered unsafe to drink without treatment. Treatment methods include use of tablets, filtering, and boiling.
- LIGHTNING—Thunderstorms occur regularly, particularly during July and August, and lightning is a real threat in the high country. During a storm, stay off mountain- or ridgetops and other exposed places, and stay out of clearings where you are the tallest object in the area. Don't seek shelter under a lone tree or under taller trees in the forest. Don't get into shallow caves or stand at the base or edge of a cliff. Safer positions are in a larger cave, crouched between rocks in a boulder field, and in forested areas. Be aware of building storms and be in a safe place before a storm arrives.
- HYPOTHERMIA—This is the leading killer of those who are ill-prepared for an outdoor experience. Most people associate hypothermia with blizzards and high-mountain conditions; in fact, most problems occur with above-freezing temperatures. This is especially true in windy or

wet conditions. Loss of body heat lowers the body's inner core temperature. Victims shiver uncontrollably and lose coordination, their speech becomes incoherent, they hallucinate and become unconscious. Death can occur in a few hours. Prevent hypothermia by recognizing its threat and planning for prevention and treatment. Proper clothing will help—a hat and wool, fleece, or polypropylene garments are best. Do not wear cotton. Drink plenty of water and eat plenty of carbohydrates. Stay dry, stay out of the wind as much as possible, dress warmly to prevent loss of body heat. Establish camp and treat hypothermia when symptoms first occur, while energy reserves exist. Symptoms include slowness, drowsiness, and shivering. Warm the body by consuming hot food and drink, by insulating with sleeping bags, with fire, and with high-energy food.

- ALTITUDE SICKNESS—It may severely affect those who live at elevations below 3,000 feet. Severe headaches, nausea, lack of appetite, sleeplessness, chest pain, shortness of breath, and dizziness may affect unacclimated people at higher elevations. Spend at least a day or two getting acclimated before hiking or undertaking more strenuous exercise. If these symptoms are present, eat quick-energy food such as fruit, nuts, candy, or fruit juice; drink plenty of fluids; avoid caffeine and alcohol. If symptoms persist, return to lower elevations. If you are on horseback, let your stock get acclimated to the altitude also. Take frequent breaks and don't push stock.
- GETTING LOST—As with all back-country situations, the Pecos Wilderness presents many opportunities for not knowing where you are (or getting lost). Panic can easily set in and a situation can quickly turn from discomforting to deadly. Knowing where you are on your map at all times and using your own abilities and common sense are the best tools you have for preventing this disconcerting and potentially dangerous situation. Remember that three yells—or three of anything— is the international signal of distress. Responsibility for search and rescue lies with the New Mexico State Police. Leave your itinerary with someone who can call them if there is a true emergency. *Search and Rescue Phone Number: (505) 827-9228.*

The Pecos Wilderness is not a city park; an injury that would be minor in town could be a major emergency in a wilderness of this size. People planning to visit a wilderness are responsible for personally assessing the conditions which might be encountered and their ability to cope with these conditions. All wilderness travel involves some degree of risk, and persons engaging in this activity assume any risk associated with it.

The maps accompanying the trail descriptions are for orientation only. For a more detailed representation of topographic features, please refer to the wilderness map or appropriate USGS quadrangles.

For more information on the Pecos Wilderness or on Santa Fe and Carson national forests, please contact:

CARSON NATIONAL FOREST
Supervisor's Office
208 Cruz Alta Road
Taos, NM 87571
505/758-6292

Camino Real Ranger District
P.O. Box 348
Peñasco, NM 87553
505/587-2255

SANTA FE NATIONAL FOREST
Supervisor's Office
1220 St. Francis Drive
Santa Fe, NM 87504
505/988-6940

Pecos Ranger District
P.O. Box 429
Pecos, NM 87552
505/757-6121

Española Ranger District
P.O. Box R
Española, NM 87532
505/753-7331

Las Vegas Ranger District
1926 N. Seventh Street
Las Vegas, NM 87701
505/425-3534

Southwest Natural and Cultural
Heritage Association
Drawer E
Albuquerque, NM 87103
505/345-9498

In case of emergencies, please contact:

Forest Fire Number—
.... 505/988-6900

Pecos Village Marshall—
.... 505/757-6444

San Miguel County Sheriff—
.... 505/425-7589

Santa Fe County Sheriff—
.... 505/984-5055

Mora County Sheriff—
.... 505/387-2222

Taos County Sheriff—
.... 505/758-3361

Rio Arriba County Sheriff—
.... 505/753-3320

State Police—
.... 505/827-2551
.... 505/827-9126

CHAMBERS OF COMMERCE

Las Vegas—
.... 505/425-8631

Santa Fe—
.... 505/983-7317

Española—
.... 505/753-2831

Taos—
.... 505/758-3873

T R A I L S

CENTRAL SECTION
TRAILHEADS

Trailheads are not patrolled. Do not leave valuable items in your vehicle. Do not leave your vehicle parked unattended for extended periods of time. You may wish to arrange shuttles or drop-offs. If your vehicle is broken into or vandalized, notify the Forest Service and the county sheriff.

ASPEN VISTA and SANTA FE SKI BASIN: From Santa Fe, follow the signs to Hyde Park and the ski basin. Aspen Vista is a small parking and picnic area just 1½ miles south of Santa Fe Ski Basin. Forest Road 150, the long, winding dirt road to the top of Tesuque Peak and the start of Trail 251 is closed to motor vehicles. You may wish to reach this trail from Santa Fe Ski Basin Trailhead. The trailhead to Trail 254 is located at the northwest end of the ski basin parking lot. *Access to Trails 251 and 254; Trail 403 (see Western Section) is nearby off 254.*

JACKS CREEK: Take State Hwy. 63 north from the town of Pecos to Jacks Creek Campground. The trailhead parking lot and horse camping area turnoff is located 100 ft. before the campground turnoff. Trailhead parking is located at the far southeast section, and the trailhead is on the east side of the parking area. Water, outhouses, corrals, picnic tables, and camping are available; a camping fee is charged. The last 9 miles of road from Terrero are unpaved. *Access to Trails 25 and 249; 257 is nearby.*

IRON GATE: Take State Hwy. 63 north from Pecos. About 5 miles north of Terrero, go 4 miles on Forest Road 223 to Iron Gate Campground. Parking is available on the south and northwest ends of the campground in the areas designated Wilderness Parking. Outhouses, corrals, picnic tables, and camping are available at the campground; no water and no camping fee. This is a rough and rocky dirt road accessible to most vehicles in good weather. Four-wheel drive may be required during wet and inclement weather. The highway is unpaved from Terrero north to Iron Gate Road. *Access to Trails 249 and 250; 248 is nearby, with its trailhead about 1 mile before Iron Gate Campground on FR 223.*

PANCHUELA: Take State Highway 63 north from Pecos to Cowles. Turn left, cross the Pecos River bridge and turn north up Forest Road 305 to Panchuela Campground. Drive 1 mile to the campground and park at the wilderness parking area. Walk through the campground and cross the Panchuela Creek bridge to the trail. Water, outhouses, picnic tables, and camping are available; a camping fee is charged. Horse trailers are not allowed at the trailhead or the campground. Trailer parking is available at Cowles. The last mile of road is rough and rocky, but accessible to most vehicles in good weather. The road becomes very slick and muddy in wet weather. *Access to Trails 259 and 288.*

COWLES: Take State Hwy. 63 north from Pecos to Cowles. Turn west at

Cowles and cross the bridge over the Pecos River. Parking is available on the west side of the bridge. Look for a trail climbing up the hillside. No facilities available. *Access to Trails 271 and 254.*

HOLY GHOST: Take State Hwy. 63 north from Pecos. Just before the bridge at Terrero, turn west on Forest Road 122 to Holy Ghost Campground. The trailhead is found just before the entrance. Water, picnic tables, outhouses, and camping are available; a fee is charged. Horse trailers are not allowed at the trailhead or the campground. Trailer parking is available at Terrero. FR 122 is a narrow, paved road with turnouts. *Access to Trail 283.*

ELK MOUNTAIN: From Pecos, take State Hwy. 63 north to Forest Road 645, Elk Mountain Road, and follow the signs to Elk Mountain Trailhead. This is a very rough and rocky dirt road and may be inaccessible during wet weather. Limited parking is available. *Access to Trail 251; 218 (not described) and 216 are nearby.*

MORA CAMPGROUND: From Pecos, take State Hwy. 63 north to Mora Campground at the junction of the Mora and Pecos rivers. Avoid parking in any of the designated overnight sites. Camping is available for a fee. No other facilities. Trail begins at the far end of the campground. *Access to Trail 240.*

EL PORVENIR: From Las Vegas, take State Hwy. 65 (Hot Springs Boulevard) northwest to United World College and through Gallinas Canyon. Follow the signs to El Porvenir Campground. Trailhead parking is available just before entering the campground. This road is paved all the way, but is narrow and curved, so drive defensively. *Access to Trails 223 and 247.*

SAPELLO: From Las Vegas, take State Hwy. 3 past Storrie Lake to Sapello. Turn left onto State Hwy. 94 and be alert for the San Ignacio turnoff. Follow State Hwy. 266 to the end of the pavement at San Ignacio and continue west along the dirt and gravel road for 6 to 7 miles. You are on private property, so stay on the road. A sign marks the turnoff for parking just south of the road next to a corral. *Access to Trail 214; from there to 223.*

WALKER FLATS: From Las Vegas, take State Hwy. 3 north to Mora and Cleveland; in Cleveland, find the sign directing you west to the national forest boundary. Follow signs about 10 miles to Walker Flats. The last 2 miles require 4-wheel drive in wet weather. At Walker Flats meadow, take the first fork left for about 1 mile. Pulloffs are available before the Rio la Casa crossing; trailhead and roads are not signed. Once past Walker Flats, there is virtually nowhere to turn a trailer around. Forest and wilderness maps do not show correct locations of roads in this area; not recommended for passenger cars. *Access to Trails 266 and 269.*

LAS DISPENSAS: From Las Vegas, take State Hwy. 3 north past Storrie Lake to Las Dispensas Road, about 10 miles north of Las Vegas. Follow this to Las Dispensas Cemetery. From here a primitive road continues another couple of miles to the trailhead. Avoid driving this road during wet weather; not recommended for passenger cars. *Access to Trail 220.*

GASCON: From Las Vegas, take State Hwy. 3 north to State Hwy. 94; follow 94 to State Hwy. 105; take 105 to its end north of Gascon. The trailhead is on private property; leave vehicles only with permission from the landowner. This trailhead is used mostly by cattlemen and hunters. *Access to Trail 239.*

MAESTAS: To reach this trail from Maestas Canyon, permission must be obtained via the Forest Service (Las Vegas office) to travel through the private land of the Martinez ranch. Take State Hwy. 3 north to Sapello. From there take Hwy. 94 to Tierra Monte, then Hwy. 105 to Rociada, then Hwy. 276 to its end near the Lost Lake ranch. Avoid in wet weather; not recommended for passenger cars. *Access to Trail 220.*

CLOSURES: The following trails may be found on USFS wilderness maps, forest maps, and USGS topo maps, but have been closed, abandoned, or no longer exist. *Please do not use these trails:* 261, 243, 26 (central), 27, 164, 215, 274, and 380-A. These trails are closed or abandoned because of resource damage, lack of use, or safety hazards.

Beattys Flats and Pecos Falls areas are closed to camping and campfires: The area designated on the left map—bounded by the south bridge over the Pecos River, the north bridge of Rito del Padre on Trail 25, and the fence which crosses Trail 24 just north of the fork of the Pecos River and Rito del Padre—is closed to camping and campfires. The area designated on the right map—bounded approximately ¼ mile east and west of the falls, and approximately ½ mile north and south of the falls—is closed to camping and campfires. These closures are necessary to prevent soil erosion, water pollution, and damage of fragile streamside habitats.

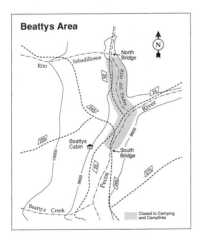

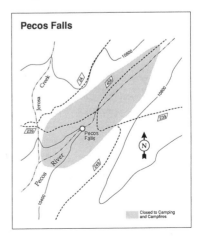

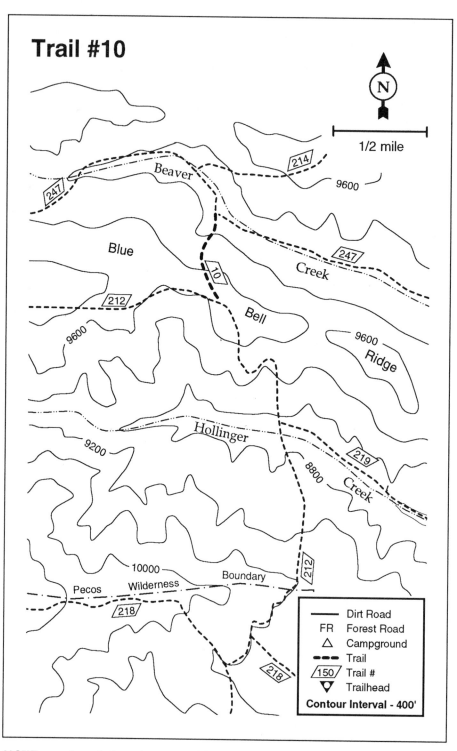

NOTE: contour intervals are at 400 feet

TRAIL 10

LENGTH: ½ mile

RATING: Difficult

USE: Light

SEASONS: Summer to fall

NOTES: **Not recommended.** The trail is very steep, rocky, and eroded; difficult to find and follow.

LOCATION: Pecos/Las Vegas Ranger District, Santa Fe National Forest

TRAIL ACCESS: Trails 247 & 212

USGS MAP: Rociada

DESCRIPTION: This short trail connects Trails 247 and 212. From Trail 247, Trail 10 takes a short, steep, rocky climb up to Blue Bell Ridge and the junction with Trail 212. The trail is eroded and may be hazardous during the rainy season.

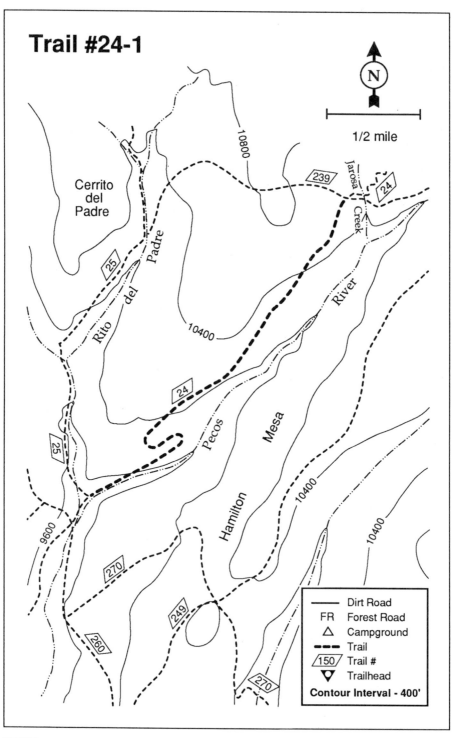

Trail #24-1

N

1/2 mile

Cerrito del Padre

10800

239

Jarosa Creek

24

25

Rito del Padre

10400

River

24

25

Pecos

Mesa

Hamilton

10400

9600

10400

270

249

260

270

	Dirt Road
FR	Forest Road
△	Campground
- - -	Trail
150	Trail #
▽	Trailhead
Contour Interval - 400'	

NOTE: contour intervals are at 400 feet

TRAIL 24, Part 1–PECOS TRAIL

LENGTH: 4 miles

RATING: Moderate

USE: Moderate

SEASONS: Late spring to early fall

HIGHEST & LOWEST POINTS: 10,560 ft. & 9,400 ft.

*NOTES: **The Beattys Flats area is closed to camping and campfires.*** Over-use has damaged this fragile environment. See closure map for exact boundaries of closure area.

LOCATION: Pecos/Las Vegas Ranger District, Santa Fe National Forest

TRAIL ACCESS: Trails 25 & 239

USGS MAP: Pecos Falls

DESCRIPTION: This is the most popular trail leading out of the Beattys area. The trail begins just north of the drift fence across the Rito del Padre bridge. Trail 24 then turns up the hillside and climbs to the top of the western ridge above the Pecos River. After this steep climb the trail maintains a moderate grade, traveling through open meadows and groves of aspen and mixed conifers. The meadows offer scenic views of the Pecos canyon area. The junction with Trail 239 is found just before crossing Jarosa Creek. Shortcuts and cow trails in this area can be confusing. Trails 239 and 24 coincide here until after crossing Jarosa Creek. Continue north and cross the creek. The second half of Trail 24 turns north at this point toward the Santa Barbara Divide, while Trail 239 continues east.

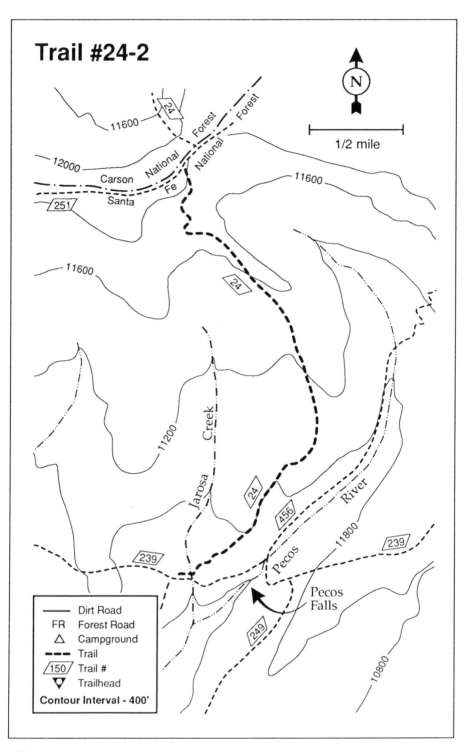

Trail #24-2

N

1/2 mile

11600

24

National Forest

National Forest

12000

Carson

Santa Fe

251

11600

11600

24

11200

Jarosa Creek

24

456

Pecos River

11800

239

239

Pecos

Pecos Falls

249

10800

Legend:

— Dirt Road
FR Forest Road
△ Campground
- - - Trail
150 Trail #
▽ Trailhead
Contour Interval - 400'

NOTE: contour intervals are at 400 feet

TRAIL 24, Part 2–PECOS TRAIL

LENGTH: 4½ miles

RATING: Moderate

USE: Light

SEASONS: Summer and fall

HIGHEST & LOWEST POINTS: 12,160 ft. & 8,960 ft.

NOTES: The trail passes through occasional meadows in which the tread may disappear.

LOCATION: Pecos/Las Vegas Ranger District, Santa Fe National Forest

TRAIL ACCESS: Trail 239 & Santa Barbara Divide

USGS MAPS: Pecos Falls, Jicarita Peak

DESCRIPTION: This section of Trail 24 is lightly used and gives the traveler a solitude-filled back-country experience. Just east of the Jarosa Creek crossing, a trail sign marks the continuation of Trail 24. This trail generally remains among the trees high on a ridge west of the Pecos drainage, occasionally passing through open meadows. The trail may disappear in meadows and you may need to search for it on the other side. Trail 24 provides a reasonably gradual climb to the top of the Santa Barbara Divide and emerges at a saddle just east of Barbara Peak. The views are excellent in all directions. The trail continues as Middle Fork Trail (see Northern Section) down the other side of the divide along the middle fork of the Rio Santa Barbara and terminates at Santa Barbara Campground.

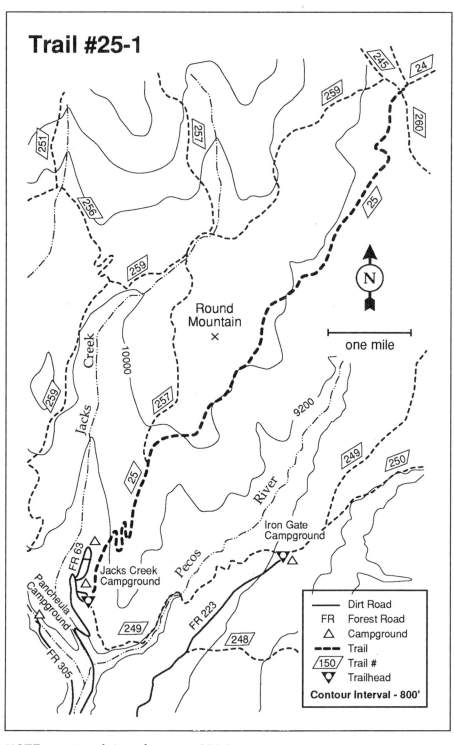

NOTE: contour intervals are at 800 feet

TRAIL 25, Part 1–BEATTYS TRAIL

LENGTH: 8 miles

RATING: Moderate

USE: Heavy

SEASONS: Late spring to late fall

HIGHEST & LOWEST POINTS: 10,160 ft. & 8,960 ft.

*NOTES: **This is one of the most heavily used trails in the wilderness.** It is popular with backpackers, day hikers, and horse riders. **The Beattys Flats area is closed to camping and campfires.** This area has been damaged by overuse. Please see closure map for exact boundaries of closure.*

LOCATION: Pecos / Las Vegas Ranger District, Santa Fe National Forest

TRAIL ACCESS: Jacks Creek Trailhead & Trail 24

USGS MAPS: Cowles, Pecos Falls

DESCRIPTION: The first mile out of Jacks Creek Trailhead is the most difficult section, with the trail gaining almost 1,000 ft. in elevation over the first 1½ miles. The grade is reasonably moderate with long switchbacks up the hillside in this first section of the trail. A major trail junction is found 2 miles up the trail with Trail 257 going north and Trail 25 continuing east. Open meadows alternate with forested areas of aspen and conifers as the trail winds across the east slope of Round Mountain and descends into the Pecos River valley. An especially fine view of the valley can be seen from the rocky cliffs just before the final descent into the Beattys Flats area. There are several trail junctions in the flats area. Trail 260 starts at the bridge across the Pecos River, Trail 259 starts ¼ mile north of that junction, and Trail 24 starts at the bridge across the Rito del Padre.

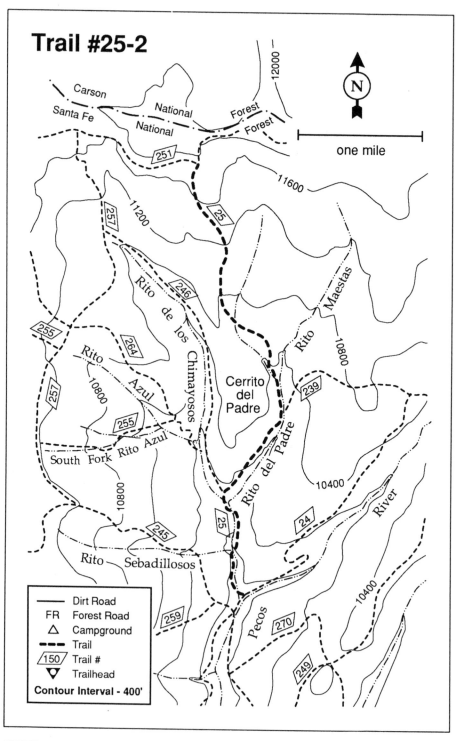

Trail #25-2

Carson National Forest

Santa Fe National Forest

one mile

12000

11600

11200

251

25

257

246

Rito de los Chimayosos

255

264

Rito Azul

10800

257

255

South Fork Rito Azul

Cerrito del Padre

Rito Maestas

10800

239

Rito del Padre

10400

10800

245

25

24

River

Rito Sebadillosos

259

Pecos

270

10400

249

Dirt Road
FR Forest Road
△ Campground
- - - Trail
/150/ Trail #
▽ Trailhead
Contour Interval - 400'

NOTE: contour intervals are at 400 feet

TRAIL 25, Part 2–BEATTYS TRAIL

LENGTH: 5 miles

RATING: Difficult

USE: Moderate

SEASONS: Summer and fall

HIGHEST & LOWEST POINTS: 12,000 ft. & 8,440 ft.

NOTES: **The Beattys Flats area is very heavily used and is closed to camping and campfires.** Please refer to closure map for exact boundaries of closure. This area has been damaged by overuse. The junction of Trails 25 and 239 along the Rito del Padre is also a popular camping spot.

LOCATION: Pecos/Las Vegas Ranger District, Santa Fe National Forest

TRAIL ACCESS: Trails 24 & 251

USGS MAP: Pecos Falls

DESCRIPTION: Trail 25 turns west from the junction with Trail 24 just before the wooden footbridge over the Rito del Padre. This part of Trail 25 is less traveled and more difficult, with the first section being eroded and boggy. The trail stays in the forest, following the Rito del Padre for about 1½ miles and has two stream crossings before encountering the junction with Trail 246. Trail 25 turns northeast up the Rito del Padre, traveling across grassy meadows and dropping back down to the creek and the junction with Trail 239. Trail 25 continues north on a gradual rise through heavy forest and small boggy areas, then climbs rapidly up the hillside to the Santa Barbara Divide and the junction with Trail 251. Excellent views of the wilderness and the surrounding country await hikers at the divide.

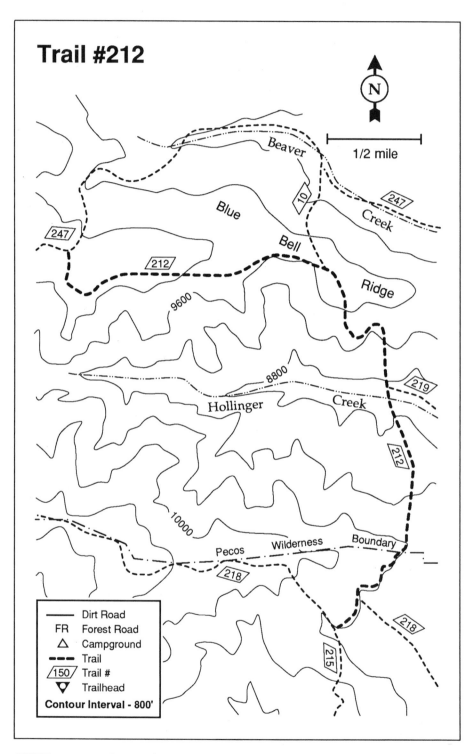

NOTE: contour intervals are at 800 feet

TRAIL 212–BLUE BELL RIDGE TRAIL

LENGTH: 4½ miles

RATING: Difficult

USE: Light

SEASONS: Late spring to mid-fall

HIGHEST & LOWEST POINTS: 10,160 ft. & 8,500 ft.

NOTES: Some sections along Blue Bell Ridge may be difficult to find and follow. Stay on the trail when passing through El Cielo and Harvey Ranch. Avoid trespassing. Trail 218 is best reached from the trailhead off Gallinas Canyon Road, 1 mile west of Baker Flat picnic area. This is not signed.

LOCATION: Pecos/Las Vegas Ranger District, Santa Fe National Forest

TRAIL ACCESS: Trails 218 & 247

USGS MAPS: Rociada, Elk Mountain

DESCRIPTION: From Trail 218 at Harvey Ranch (and junction with Trail 215), go north to Hollinger Creek. After a short level section the trail will begin to drop down into the Hollinger canyon. Open meadows characterize the area around Hollinger Creek. Trail 212 crosses to the north side of the creek and heads up to Blue Bell Ridge. This section of trail is extremely steep, climbing 1,200 ft. in 1½ miles. The trail levels out at the top of the ridge before meeting Trail 10. Trail 212 continues along the top of the ridge to the west. Rocky sections can make it difficult to find the trail. Near the end of Blue Bell Ridge the trail turns north and ends at Trail 247.

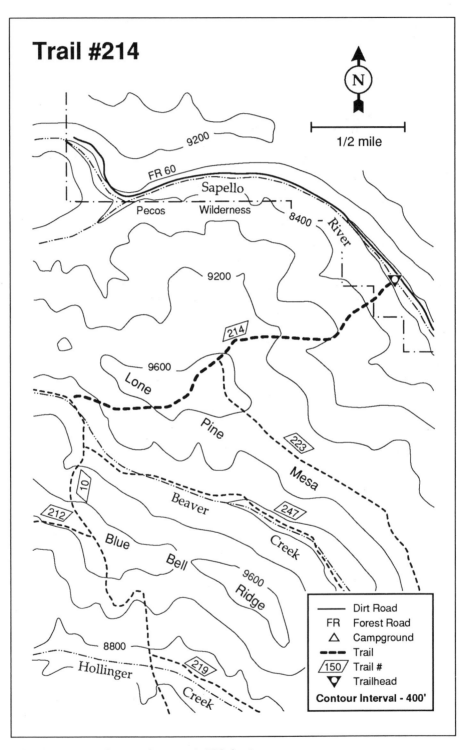

Trail #214

N

1/2 mile

9200

FR 60

Sapello

Pecos   Wilderness

8400   River

9200

214

9600

Lone

Pine

223

Mesa

10

Beaver

212

247

Blue

Bell   Creek

9600

Ridge

8800

Hollinger   219

Creek

	Dirt Road
FR	Forest Road
△	Campground
- - -	Trail
/150/	Trail #
▽	Trailhead
Contour Interval - 400'	

NOTE: contour intervals are at 400 feet

TRAIL 214–LONE PINE MESA TRAIL

LENGTH: 3 miles

RATING: Difficult

USE: Light

SEASONS: Late spring to mid-fall

HIGHEST & LOWEST POINTS: 9,680 ft. & 8,000 ft.

NOTES: The trail is surrounded by private property for the first ½ mile. Do not trespass.

LOCATION: Pecos / Las Vegas Ranger District, Santa Fe National Forest

TRAIL ACCESS: Forest Road 60 & Trail 247

USGS MAP: Rociada

DESCRIPTION: From FR 60, cross the Sapello River and continue up the trail between the fenced private land to either side. The trail begins to switchback up the hillside, leveling out occasionally along plateaus and soon entering the meadows of Lone Pine Mesa. The trail intersects with Trail 223 after 1½ miles at the top of the ridge and continues west. It drops quickly down into Beaver Creek and the intersection with Trail 247.

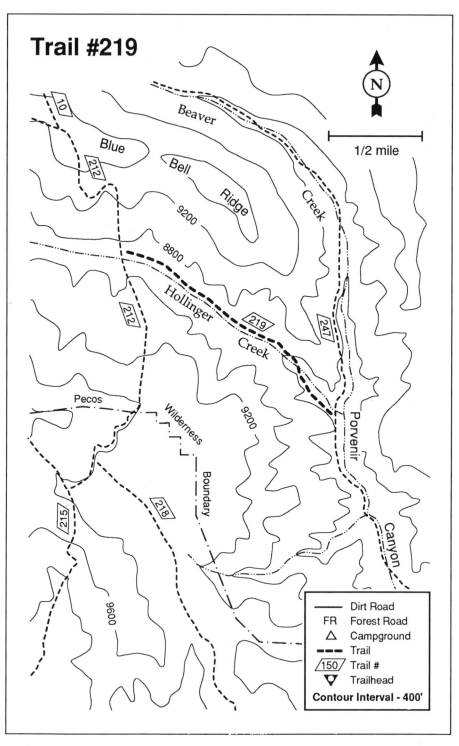

NOTE: contour intervals are at 400 feet

TRAIL 219–HOLLINGER TRAIL

LENGTH: 2 miles

RATING: Difficult

USE: Light

SEASONS: Late spring to mid-fall

HIGHEST & LOWEST POINTS: 8,560 ft. & 8,200 ft.

NOTES: The trail intersections may be difficult to find. This area is lightly used and provides good opportunities for solitude.

LOCATION: Pecos/Las Vegas Ranger District, Santa Fe National Forest

TRAIL ACCESS: Trails 247 & 212

USGS MAP: Rociada

DESCRIPTION: From the junction with Trail 247 at Beaver Creek, Trail 219 travels up the meadows alongside Hollinger Creek. The trail crosses the stream many times in the 2 miles before the junction with Trail 212. This intersection may be difficult to find because of the light use which makes the trail hard to follow.

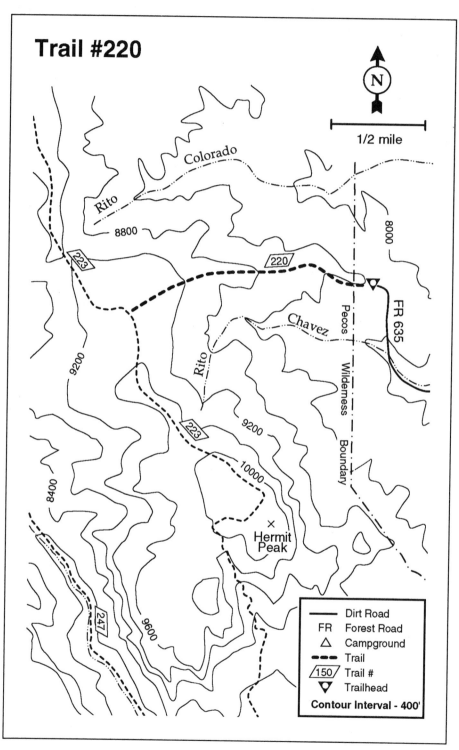

Trail #220

N

1/2 mile

Rito Colorado

8800

223

220

8000

9200

Rito

Chavez

Pecos Wilderness Boundary

FR 635

223

9200

10000

8400

×
Hermit
Peak

247

9600

———		Dirt Road
FR		Forest Road
△		Campground
- - -		Trail
150		Trail #
▽		Trailhead

Contour Interval - 400'

NOTE: contour intervals are at 400 feet

TRAIL 220

LENGTH: 2 miles

RATING: Moderate

USE: Moderate

SEASONS: Summer to fall

NOTES: Trail not shown on USGS maps; road to trailhead is difficult during wet weather.

LOCATION: Pecos/Las Vegas Ranger District, Santa Fe National Forest

TRAIL ACCESS: Forest Road 635 & Trail 223

USGS MAP: Rociada

DESCRIPTION: This trail begins at the end of Las Dispensas Road (FR 635). The trail travels steadily uphill along a ridge between the Rito Chavez and the Rito Colorado. After traveling 2 miles through mixed conifer forest, the trail ends at the junction with Trail 223.

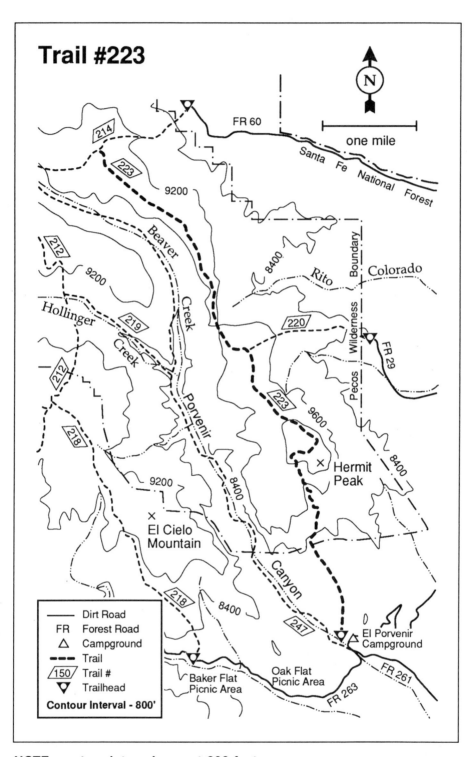

Trail #223

N

one mile

FR 60

Santa Fe National Forest

214

223

9200

Beaver

Creek

212

9200

Hollinger

219

Creek

212

Porvenir

218

9200

×
El Cielo
Mountain

8400

Rito

Colorado

Boundary

Wilderness

Pecos

220

223

9600

FR 29

8400

× Hermit
    Peak

Canyon

247

8400

218

8400

El Porvenir
Campground

FR 261

Baker Flat
Picnic Area

Oak Flat
Picnic Area

FR 263

——	Dirt Road
FR	Forest Road
△	Campground
- - -	Trail
150	Trail #
▽	Trailhead

Contour Interval - 800'

NOTE: contour intervals are at 800 feet

TRAIL 223–HERMIT PEAK TRAIL

LENGTH: 9½ miles

RATING: Moderate to difficult

USE: Heavy

SEASONS: Late spring to mid-fall

HIGHEST & LOWEST POINTS: 10,160 ft. & 7,520 ft.

NOTES: **Not recommended for horses.** The first 4 miles of this trail receives heavy use even though gaining almost 3,000 ft. in elevation. Expect a hard climb. The trail is on private land for the first 2 miles; please stay on the trail and do not trespass.

LOCATION: Pecos/Las Vegas Ranger District, Santa Fe National Forest

TRAIL ACCESS: El Porvenir Trailhead & Trail 214

USGS MAPS: El Porvenir, Rociada

DESCRIPTION: Starting from the parking lot by El Porvenir Campground, cross the bridge over the river and follow the trail back across the road through the campground. The trail passes private property when you leave the campground, traveling through open pine forests to the base of Hermit Peak. From here the trail begins a series of switchbacks up the face of the peak, maneuvering around the sheer cliffs which make a trail seem impossible from a distance. Several good views can be found along the trail as it climbs to the summit. Spur trails on the summit will take you across the top of this flat mountain to spectacular views. Trail 223 continues north and west across Hermit Peak and then begins a steep descent for about a mile. It then levels out and goes northwest along a ridge off the peak. The trail travels through forested areas along this ridge and Lone Pine Mesa for 6 miles and then enters a meadow. The trail may be difficult to find in this area, but soon reaches the junction with Trail 214 near the top of Lone Pine Mesa.

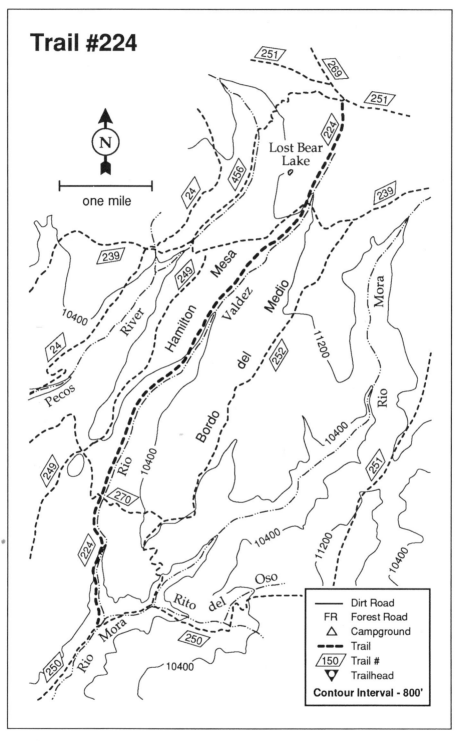

NOTE: contour intervals are at 800 feet

TRAIL 224–VALDEZ TRAIL

LENGTH: 9 miles

RATING: Moderate

USE: Moderate

SEASONS: Summer through fall

HIGHEST & LOWEST POINTS: 11,800 ft. & 9,300 ft.

NOTES: This trail offers a relatively easy yet less traveled route into the Pecos back country; a good trail for those seeking solitude.

LOCATION: Pecos/Las Vegas Ranger District, Santa Fe National Forest

TRAIL ACCESS: Trails 250 & 251

USGS MAPS: Pecos Falls, Elk Mountain

DESCRIPTION: This relatively easy trail takes off from Trail 250 at the junction of the Rio Valdez and Rio Mora. Trail 224 offers one of the most gradual climbs to the top of the Santa Barbara Divide, with the 2,500-ft. climb spread out evenly over 9 miles. The trail follows the west bank of the Valdez, passing through mixed conifer forests and crossing the river several times in the first 2 miles. The canyon then broadens into open meadows. At this point you will find the junction with Trail 270. This area is popular with cattle; expect to see them grazing here. Trail 224 continues north along the Valdez, paralleling the river and passing through meadows and forests. At mile 7 you will encounter the junction with Trail 239. 224 continues up the river valley, occasionally becoming difficult to follow in the marshy meadows. The trail ends on the Santa Barbara Divide at the intersection with Trail 251 and near the convergence with Trails 456 and 269.

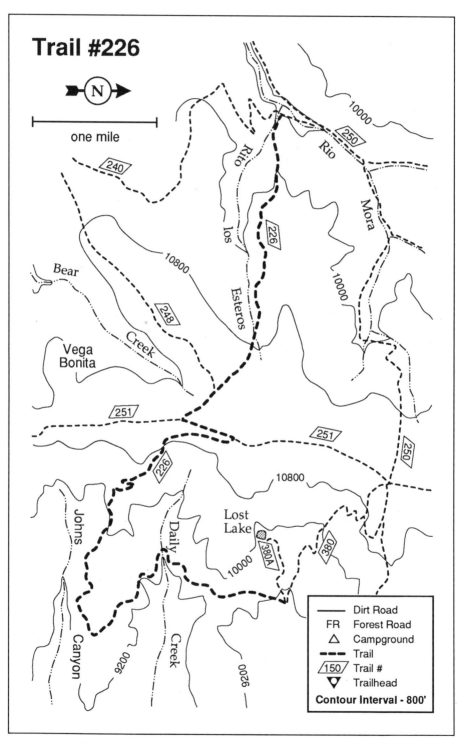

NOTE: contour intervals are at 800 feet

TRAIL 226–ESTEROS TRAIL

LENGTH: 10 miles

RATING: Difficult

USE: Light

SEASONS: Summer to mid-fall

HIGHEST & LOWEST POINTS: 11,040 ft. & 9,120 ft.

NOTES: This trail is lightly used and will be difficult to find and follow in the large meadows near the top of the divide. Tree fall may make this trail difficult for livestock travel.

LOCATION: Pecos/Las Vegas Ranger District, Santa Fe National Forest

TRAIL ACCESS: Trails 240 & 380

USGS MAP: Elk Mountain

DESCRIPTION: Trail 226 provides a steep, eroded, and rocky climb toward the eastern divide with good views of the surrounding country. The trail traverses open meadows, aspen groves, and mixed conifer forests. From the junction of Trails 250 and 240 in Mora Flats, take Trail 240 across the Rio Mora. The trail crosses through a meadow and heads toward the treeline. Due to light use, the trail may be difficult to follow in the meadow. Trail 226 branches off from Trail 240 where 240 crosses the Rito los Esteros. From this junction, 226 switchbacks up the southwest face of the Esteros canyon. Just across the canyon to the west the large, open meadows of Hamilton Mesa can be seen. As the trail approaches the eastern divide, the terrain levels out somewhat, with a thick spruce forest and lush undergrowth providing a scenic passage. The trail branches out in a large meadow near the top of the divide, with most of these spurs fading out in the boggy sections of the meadow. Visitors should continue east to the top of the meadow and then turn slightly south, looking for a marker indicating the continuation of Trail 226. The trail continues to the northeast in the trees skirting the head end of a canyon to the south, then heads southeast to the junction with Trail 251. Continue north on 251 for ½ mile at which point Trail 226 branches southeast, then heads north to its terminus at Trail 380.

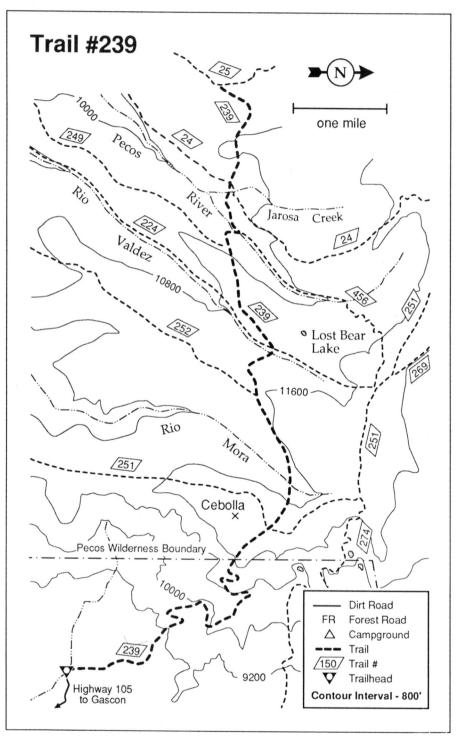

Trail #239

N

one mile

25

239

24

249

10000

Pecos

River

Jarosa Creek

24

224

Valdez

Rio

10800

456

251

252

239

Lost Bear
Lake

269

11600

251

Rio

Mora

251

Cebolla
×

274

Pecos Wilderness Boundary

10000

239

Highway 105
to Gascon

9200

Dirt Road
FR   Forest Road
△   Campground
- - -   Trail
150   Trail #
▽   Trailhead
Contour Interval - 800'

NOTE: contour intervals are at 800 feet

TRAIL 239–GASCON TRAIL

LENGTH: 6½ miles

RATING: Difficult

USE: Moderate

SEASONS: Late spring to mid-fall

HIGHEST & LOWEST POINTS: 11,760 ft. & 10,100 ft.

NOTES: On this short section of trail, the climb is steep and the trail is badly eroded. This trail receives heavy use during hunting season. ***The Pecos Falls area is closed to camping and campfires.*** Please see closure map for exact boundaries of closure area. This area has been damaged by overuse.

LOCATION: Pecos/Las Vegas Ranger District, Santa Fe National Forest

TRAIL ACCESS: Trail 25 & Gascon

USGS MAPS: Pecos Falls, Gascon

DESCRIPTION: The trail crosses three ridges and three major drainages, crosses the eastern divide to Gascon Point, and drops into the town of Gascon. The first section of trail heads east from the junction with Trail 25 through a large meadow. This section is badly eroded and takes a short, steep climb over the ridge between the Rito del Padre and Jarosa Creek. Multiple trails have developed over the years as previous trails have become unusable due to erosion. The trail enters the trees at the top of the ridge and continues to the junction with Trail 24 near Jarosa Creek. The two trails are the same until after the creek crossing. Trail 239 then continues eastward and intersects with Trail 456 near Pecos Falls. The falls are a scenic cascade in the Pecos River, with water tumbling over a series of stair-stepped rocks. This area is restricted to day use only. The trail crosses the Pecos River going northeast to the junction with Trail 224. This section of trail passes through spruce forests and is very rocky. After crossing the Valdez, Trail 239 begins the climb to the top of the Bordo del Medio Mesa and the junction with Trail 252. 239 continues in a northeasterly direction across the Bordo before descending to the headwaters of the Rio Mora in a wide meadow at the corner of the Santa Barbara and eastern divides. A short, easy climb up the east slope brings the traveler to the top of the eastern divide and Trail 251. From here, Trail 239 continues south and east across the divide to Gascon Point and then descends down the other side to its terminus at the town of Gascon, 6 miles to the east. This section of trail is steep, rocky, eroded, and dangerous to livestock travel.

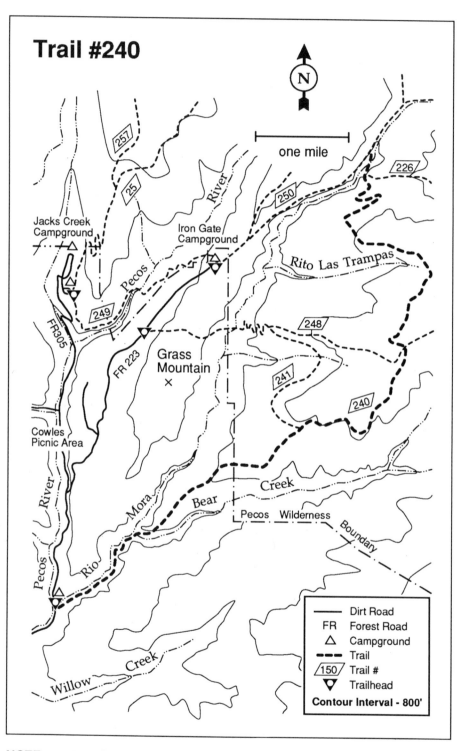

NOTE: contour intervals are at 800 feet

TRAIL 240–LAS TRAMPAS TRAIL

LENGTH: 9½ miles

RATING: Difficult

USE: Light

SEASONS: Late spring to early fall

HIGHEST & LOWEST POINTS: 10,560 ft. & 7,960 ft.

NOTES: This is a lightly used trail traversing some of the more remote areas of the Pecos Wilderness. In late spring and after periods of heavy rain, the Rio Mora can be dangerous to cross. Hikers should be prepared for wet feet as the trail crosses the river fourteen times in the first 2 miles. Secondary trails up the river from the campground may make it difficult to find the main trail. The trail can be lost occasionally in open meadows and where livestock trails intersect the main trail.

LOCATION: Pecos/Las Vegas Ranger District, Santa Fe National Forest

TRAIL ACCESS: Mora Campground & Trail 250

USGS MAPS: Elk Mountain, Cowles

DESCRIPTION: Trail 240 makes a steep, rocky ascent up the Rio Mora canyon to the high mountain meadows of the Pecos back country. The trail begins after the last campsite in Mora Campground where the road narrows into a trail. After the final crossing of the Rio Mora, the trail climbs up the hillside to a gate. After passing through the gate and crossing Bear Creek, you may see a post marking the trail up out of the canyon. Secondary trails continue along the river, but Trail 240 begins the rapid and rocky climb out of the canyon at this point. The trail levels out when it reaches the ridge above the canyon and continues along the ridge at a good pitch. Small clearings are encountered just before the trail emerges into a vast, open clearing and the junction with Trail 241. From this point continue along the large, open meadow 2 miles to the junction with Trail 248. From here you will hike through dense forest, cross the head of the Rito las Trampas and begin descending into the Mora valley. The junction with Trail 226 is found after crossing the Rito los Esteros. The trail continues for another ½ mile to its terminus at Trail 250.

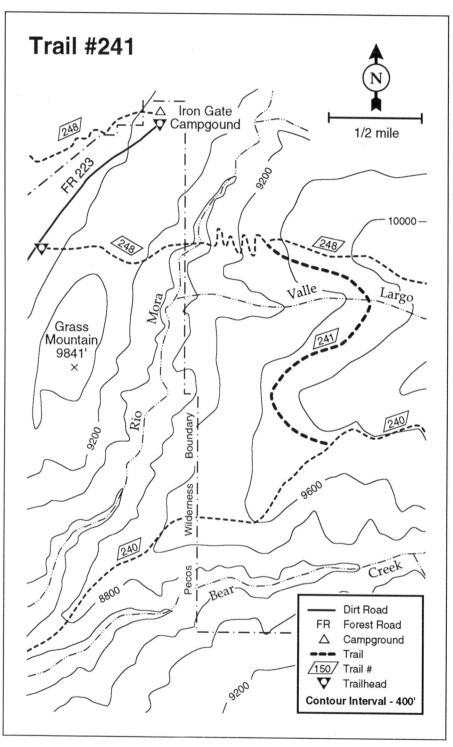

NOTE: contour intervals are at 400 feet

TRAIL 241

LENGTH: 2¼ miles

RATING: Moderate

USE: Moderate

SEASONS: Summer to fall

NOTES: The trail is obscure in places, especially the meadows; junctions are difficult to find.

LOCATION: Pecos/Las Vegas Ranger District, Santa Fe National Forest

TRAIL ACCESS: Trails 248 & 240

USGS MAP: Elk Mountain

DESCRIPTION: The trail is easy to find at its junction with Trail 248. The trail goes from Valle Largo to Valle Medio. Trail 241 travels through forested areas interspersed with meadows before entering Valle Medio. The junction with Trail 240 in Valle Medio is difficult to find.

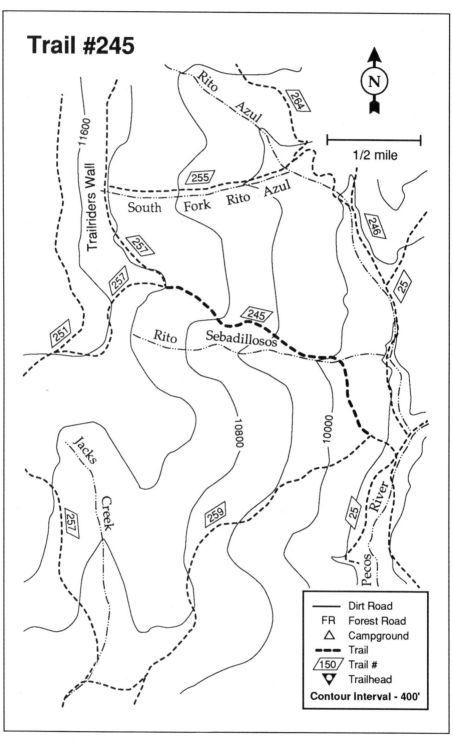

Trail #245

N

1/2 mile

Rito Azul

264

11600

Trailriders Wall

255

South Fork Rito Azul

246

257

257

25

245

251

Rito Sebadillosos

Jacks

Creek

10800

10000

257

259

25

Pecos River

	Dirt Road
FR	Forest Road
△	Campground
- - -	Trail
150	Trail #
▽	Trailhead
Contour Interval - 400'	

NOTE: contour intervals are at 400 feet

TRAIL 245–SEBADILLOSOS TRAIL

LENGTH: 2½ miles

RATING: Difficult

USE: Moderate

SEASONS: Summer to early fall

HIGHEST & LOWEST POINTS: 11,200 ft. & 9,720 ft.

NOTES: Not recommended for horses. This trail is extremely steep, eroded, and difficult. Large boggy areas are difficult and unsafe to cross, especially for livestock. The trail gets very slick when wet.

LOCATION: Pecos / Las Vegas Ranger District, Santa Fe National Forest

TRAIL ACCESS: Trails 259 & 257

USGS MAPS: Pecos Falls, Truchas Peak

DESCRIPTION: From the Beattys Flats area, go to the junction of Trails 25 and 259 approximately ¼ mile north of the Pecos River bridge. The trail branches off the hillside west of the flats and south of Rito Sebadillosos. After a steep climb to a bench above the flats, one comes to the junction with Trail 259. Trail 245 branches off to the right, winds through dense timber, and crosses the Sebadillosos drainage. After crossing the creek, the trail climbs its way up the slope through timber and occasional bogs for another ½ mile before emerging into the open meadows at the head end of the Sebadillosos drainage. Some of the worst problems with drainage and erosion occur along this stretch as the trail climbs quickly up the open meadow. A treacherous bog marks the start of the steep ascent to the top of the ridge between the Rito Azul and Sebadillosos drainages and the junction with Trail 257. Views of the surrounding country are magnificent from the head of the drainage and from the top of Trailriders Wall. Trail 245 ends here and you can continue north or southwest on Trail 257, but the climb from the junction with Trail 257 is narrow and rocky, and often stays snow covered until July. When wet, icy, or snow-covered, this section of trail is dangerous.

This trail is scheduled for reconstruction in the summer of 1991. Please check with the Pecos / Las Vegas office for progress and new location.

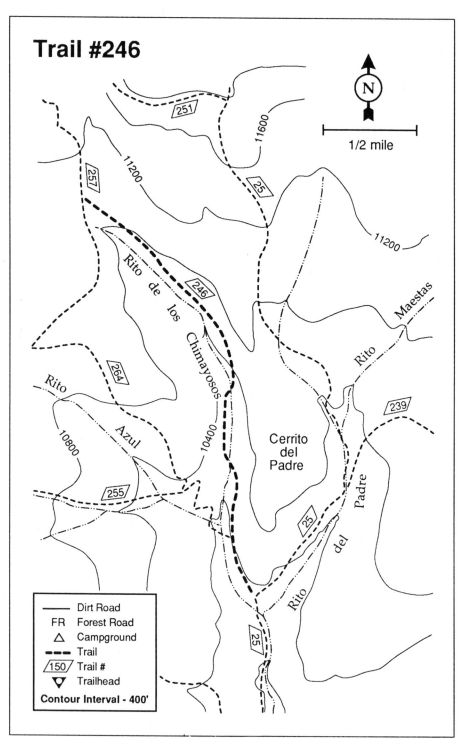

Trail #246

N

1/2 mile

251

11600

11200

257

25

11200

Rito de los Chimayosos

246

Maestas

264

Rito

Rito

239

Rito

Azul

10800

Cerrito del Padre

10400

255

25

Rito del Padre

25

	Dirt Road
FR	Forest Road
△	Campground
- - -	Trail
150	Trail #
▽	Trailhead
Contour Interval - 400'	

NOTE: contour intervals are at 400 feet

TRAIL 246–CHIMAYOSOS TRAIL

LENGTH: 3½ miles

RATING: Difficult

USE: Light

SEASONS: Summer to mid-fall

HIGHEST & LOWEST POINTS: 10,960 ft. & 9,840 ft.

*NOTES: **Not recommended.*** This route is lightly used and the trail can be difficult to find and follow. This trail is not shown on USGS maps and is very difficult to find from the north end. Recommended for experienced hikers with good map and compass skills.

LOCATION: Pecos/Las Vegas Ranger District, Santa Fe National Forest

TRAIL ACCESS: Trails 25 & 257

USGS MAPS: Pecos Falls, Truchas Peak

DESCRIPTION: Chimayosos Trail has a reasonably uniform grade and is a good route for those seeking solitude and a more challenging experience. From Beattys Flats, follow Trail 25 up the Rito del Padre 1 mile to Trail 246. Turn west up the Azul drainage and proceed upstream for ½ mile. Near the junction of the Rito Azul and the Rito de los Chimayosos, Trail 246 continues up the east side of the Chimayosos. The trail passes through spruce forest and meadows, making two stream crossings in the next mile. Continue up the east side, crossing meadows with outstanding views of the Truchas Peaks. After a couple of miles, you will turn away from the drainage. The trail then passes through a wooded area where the tread may be difficult to find and follow. The intersection with Trail 257 is soon encountered and the trail becomes more obvious.

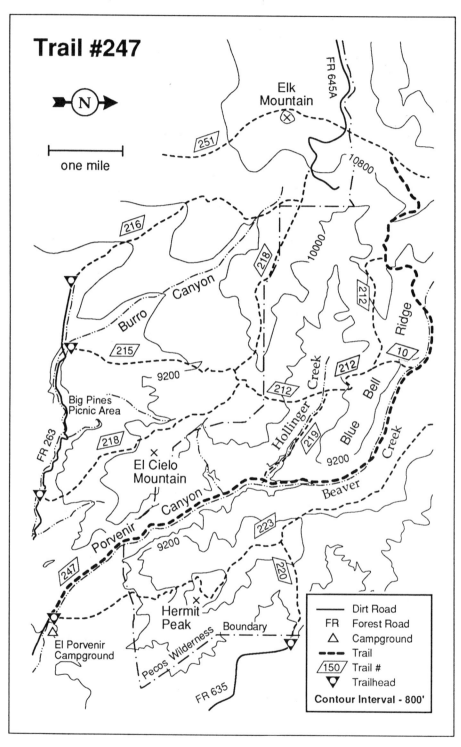

Trail #247

N

one mile

Elk Mountain ⊗

FR 645A

251

10800

216

218

10000

212

Burro Canyon

Ridge

215

9200

212

10

Big Pines Picnic Area

212

Hollinger Creek

Blue Bell

FR 263

218

219

Creek

El Cielo Mountain ×

9200

Beaver

Porvenir Canyon

9200

223

247

220

Hermit Peak ×

Boundary

El Porvenir Campground

Pecos Wilderness

FR 635

	Dirt Road
FR	Forest Road
△	Campground
- - -	Trail
150	Trail #
▽	Trailhead
Contour Interval – 800'	

NOTE: contour intervals are at 800 feet

TRAIL 247–PORVENIR CANYON TRAIL

LENGTH: 13 miles

RATING: Moderate

USE: Moderate

SEASONS: Late spring to mid-fall

HIGHEST & LOWEST POINTS: 11,280 ft. & 7,520 ft.

NOTES: The first 5-mile section of this trail is used extensively by day hikers. The trail crosses El Porvenir Creek twenty-three times in the first 5 miles, so be prepared to get your feet wet! ***High spring runoff can make the trail inaccessible and dangerous.***

LOCATION: Pecos/Las Vegas Ranger District, Santa Fe National Forest

TRAIL ACCESS: El Porvenir Trailhead & Trail 251

USGS MAPS: El Porvenir, Rociada, Elk Mountain

DESCRIPTION: Porvenir Canyon is a spectacular, scenic canyon. The cliffs of Hermit Peak and those of El Cielo Mountain can be seen to either side of the trail. During the wet season, waterfalls can be seen pouring down the sheer face of Hermit Peak. From the trailhead, Trail 247 passes through private property for 2 miles. Please stay on the trail to avoid trespassing. The trail continues up the canyon, jumping back and forth across the creek. In this section, spectacular cliffs tower above the canyon. This scenic stretch continues for almost 5 miles to the intersection of Hollinger and Beaver creeks. Trail 247 continues up Beaver Creek through open meadows. After about 4 miles the junction with Trail 10 is encountered. At this point the trail begins a steep ascent out of the canyon to the top of the eastern divide. The trail can become hard to find and follow in the meadows just before the top. Trail 247 reaches its terminus at Trail 251 at the top of the divide, with wonderful views of the surrounding area.

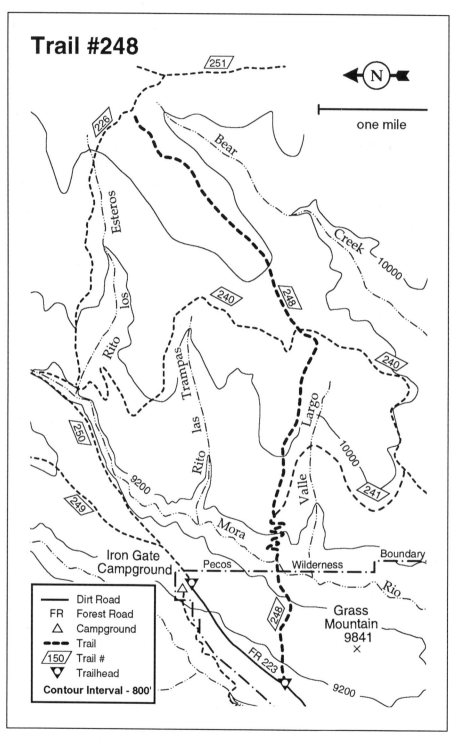

NOTE: contour intervals are at 800 feet

TRAIL 248–VALLE LARGO TRAIL

LENGTH: 6¾ miles

RATING: Moderate

USE: Moderate

SEASONS: Summer to fall

NOTES: Trail may be hard to find in meadows; cow trails may obscure main trail. Avoid being in meadows or other open areas during thunderstorms. High water can make the Rio Mora crossing hazardous.

LOCATION: Pecos/Las Vegas Ranger District, Santa Fe National Forest

TRAIL ACCESS: Forest Road 223 & Trail 226

USGS MAP: Elk Mountain

DESCRIPTION: The trail begins on Iron Gate Road, about 1½ miles south of Iron Gate Trailhead. The trail climbs around the north side of Grass Mountain and then switchbacks down to the Rio Mora. These switchbacks are not shown on the Forest Service wilderness map. This crossing is difficult; you will get your feet wet. The trail ascends out of the drainage on another series of switchbacks, traveling through mixed conifer forest. The junction with Trail 241 is encountered at the top of the switchbacks. Shortly after this junction, the trail enters Valle Largo, a large meadow. The trail can be difficult to find in the grass. It follows along the north side of the meadow, meets Trail 240, and then enters the forest, making a moderate climb up a long ridge. Near the top of the ridge, the trail enters meadows again and may be obscured. About a mile farther on the trail ends at the junction with Trail 226, which may be difficult to find.

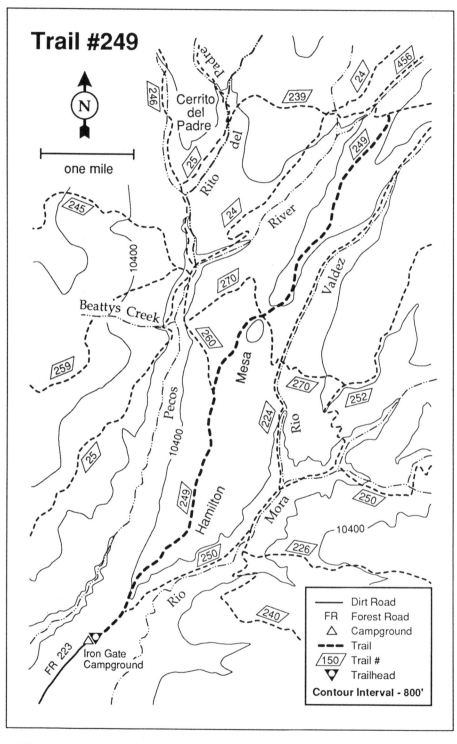

NOTE: contour intervals are at 800 feet

TRAIL 249–HAMILTON MESA TRAIL

LENGTH: 8 miles

RATING: Easy

USE: Heavy

SEASONS: Late spring to late fall

HIGHEST & LOWEST POINTS: 10,720 ft. & 9,350 ft.

NOTES: This trail receives extremely heavy use in the first few miles from hikers out of the Iron Gate Campground. ***The Pecos Falls and Beattys Flats areas are closed to camping and campfires.*** Overuse of these areas has caused severe resource damage. Please see closure map for exact boundaries of closure area. There is not much water along this trail. High, exposed terrain makes this trail dangerous during lightning storms.

LOCATION: Pecos/Las Vegas Ranger District, Santa Fe National Forest

TRAIL ACCESS: Iron Gate Campground & Trail 239

USGS MAPS: Elk Mountain, Pecos Falls

DESCRIPTION: This popular trail provides an easy, gradual incline with outstanding views, and is an excellent trail for the novice hiker. From Iron Gate Campground, the trail climbs to the top of Hamilton Mesa in the first 2 miles. The open meadows of Hamilton Mesa offer a panorama of the Pecos country and its high mountain peaks. The junction with Trail 250 is encountered ½ mile from the campground. The trail goes through open meadows interrupted by short sections of conifer forests. Trail 260 branches south at 3½ miles and Trail 270 is encountered 1 mile later. The trail then shifts to the east side of the mesa, drops down into the heavy timber, and reaches its terminus in the forest at Trail 239.

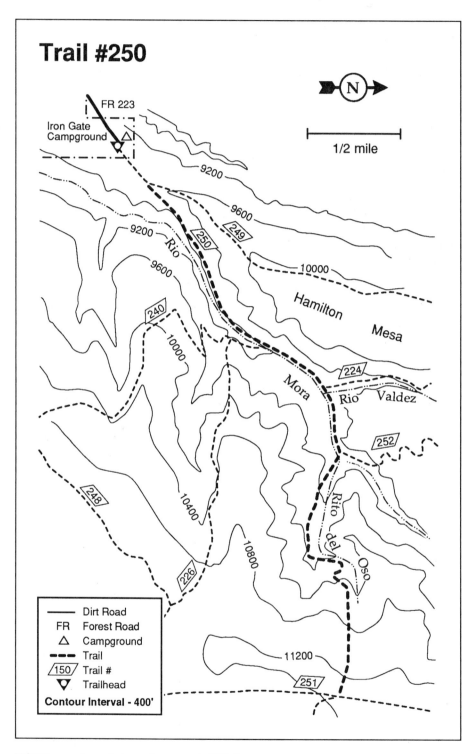

Trail #250

N

1/2 mile

FR 223

Iron Gate
Campground

9200

9600

249

9200

250

Rio

9600

10000

240

Hamilton

Mesa

10000

224

Mora

Rio

Valdez

252

248

Rito

del

10400

Oso

10800

226

11200

251

	Dirt Road
FR	Forest Road
△	Campground
---	Trail
/150/	Trail #
▽	Trailhead

Contour Interval - 400'

NOTE: contour intervals are at 400 feet

TRAIL 250–ROCIADA TRAIL

LENGTH: 8 miles

RATING: Difficult

USE: Heavy

SEASONS: Late spring to late fall

HIGHEST & LOWEST POINTS: 11,320 ft. & 9,200 ft.

*NOTES: **The first 3 miles of this trail are heavily used.*** This trail is popular with day hikers, backpackers, and horseback riders leaving from Iron Gate Campground. Mora Flats is a heavily used camping area. Please use low-impact camping methods in this area. Campers and hikers seeking solitude should hike another trail.

LOCATION: Pecos/Las Vegas Ranger District, Santa Fe National Forest

TRAIL ACCESS: Trails 249 & 251

USGS MAPS: Elk Mountain, Pecos Falls

DESCRIPTION: From Iron Gate Campground, take Trail 249. Trail 250 splits off to the right after 1 mile and drops 2 miles down the hillside through mixed conifer forests at a gentle grade to the meadows of the Rio Mora valley. The area along the river is known as Mora Flats and is an extremely popular and overused camping area. Trail 250 receives little use from this point to its terminus at Trail 251. Upon reaching the river, remain on the west bank and travel north for 1 mile to the junction of Trails 224 and 250 at the junction of the Rio Valdez and Rio Mora. Trail 250 crosses the Valdez and travels up the north bank of the Mora for a mile to the junction with Trail 252. The trail stays to the right, crossing the Rio Mora then the Rito del Oso. Trail 250 continues up the Rito del Oso, becoming increasingly rocky and steep as it climbs through the forest and out of the canyon. There are several rocky, eroded paths in the 1½-mile climb to the divide. Blazes will help you find the best path. The trail tops out and reaches its terminus at Trail 251 on the eastern divide. A large meadow at the top of the divide gives excellent views in all directions.

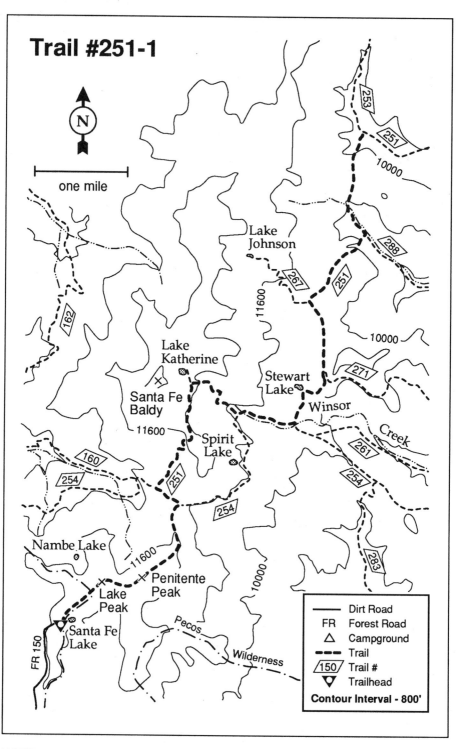

NOTE: contour intervals are at 800 feet

TRAIL 251, Part 1–SKYLINE TRAIL

LENGTH: 14 miles

RATING: Difficult

USE: Heavy

SEASONS: Summer to late fall

HIGHEST & LOWEST POINTS: 12,404 ft. and 9,760 ft.

NOTES: Forest Road 150 to the Tesuque Peak radio towers is closed to motor vehicles. You may hike, bike, or cross-country ski up the road to the trailhead, or take the chairlift from the ski basin to its terminus and walk to the radio towers. You may find it easier to reach this section of Trail 251 from Aspen Basin Trailhead and Trail 254. The section of trail from FR 150 to Penitente Peak is rocky and narrow and *inaccessible to horses.* The trail to the top of Penitente Peak is infrequently maintained and you may encounter considerable tree fall. *All lake basins in the wilderness are closed to camping and campfires. This trail is one of the most heavily used trails in the Pecos.* Those seeking solitude may wish to go to another area.

LOCATION: Española and Pecos/Las Vegas ranger districts, Santa Fe National Forest

TRAIL ACCESS: FR 150 & Trail 253

USGS MAPS: Aspen Basin, Cowles

DESCRIPTION: Skyline Trail is the longest trail in the Pecos Wilderness, traversing approximately 50 miles of ridges and passing all the way around the Pecos drainage basin. From FR 150, Trail 251 can be picked up by following along the top of the ridge to the north. A climb of 500 ft. will take the hiker to the top of Lake Peak. The trail is narrow, rocky, and hard to follow for the last ½ mile to Lake Peak. The trail continues along a narrow, rocky ridge to Penitente Peak and then follows a gentle ridge to the southern junction with Trail 254. Continue west along 254 to Puerto Nambe and the continuation of Trail 251. The trail goes north up the Santa Fe Baldy ridge. At the top of the ridge, the trail passes Lake Katherine and switchbacks down the north face. This section of trail is normally snow packed until the end of June and is hazardous when snow covered. Livestock travel is not recommended from Puerto Nambe to the junction with 254 north of Spirit Lake. The trail continues along the drainage at the far northeast corner of the lake basin and switchbacks rapidly down to Winsor Creek and follows the creek for 1 mile to another junction with 254. Trail 251 continues north on a moderate grade passing Stewart Lake and joins with Trails 271 and 267. From here the trail makes a short climb to the junction with Trail 288 and then drops steeply for 2 miles to the junction with Trail 253. This area is known as Horsethief Meadows and is another popular camping area.

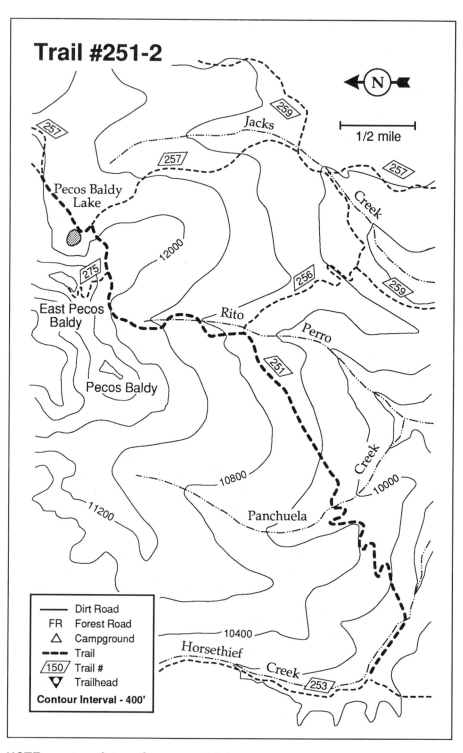

NOTE: contour intervals are at 400 feet

TRAIL 251, Part 2–SKYLINE TRAIL

LENGTH: 5 miles

RATING: Difficult

USE: Moderate

SEASONS: Early summer to late fall

HIGHEST & LOWEST POINTS: 11,840 ft. & 9,800 ft.

NOTES: Horsethief Meadow and Pecos Baldy Lake are heavily used areas. Those seeking solitude may wish to camp in another area. *All lake basins in the Pecos Wilderness are closed to camping and campfires.* These areas have been damaged by overuse. There are good campsites northeast of the lake and south along Trail 257. Bighorn sheep in the Pecos Baldy area will not hesitate to enter campsites and get into unattended supplies, so keep food out of reach. *Do not feed the sheep or any other animals.*

LOCATION: Pecos/Las Vegas Ranger District, Santa Fe National Forest

TRAIL ACCESS: Trails 253 & 257

USGS MAPS: Cowles, Truchas Peak

DESCRIPTION: At the intersection of Trails 253 and 251, follow the trail going east downstream along Horsethief Creek. After ½ mile the trail begins to climb the hillside to the north. The trail climbs steeply out of the canyon, reaches the top of a ridge, and drops quickly into Panchuela Creek. A gradual climb over the next 1½ miles brings the traveler to the intersection with Trail 256. Skyline Trail turns north and begins the long, steep, rocky climb through spruce forest to the top of Pecos Baldy ridge. The last ½ mile to the top is steep, rocky, and slightly difficult to follow. Trail 251 descends the north face of the ridge to the Pecos Baldy Lake basin and the junction with Trail 257. This last section of trail can stay snow covered until July and is very muddy and slippery during snow melt and rains.

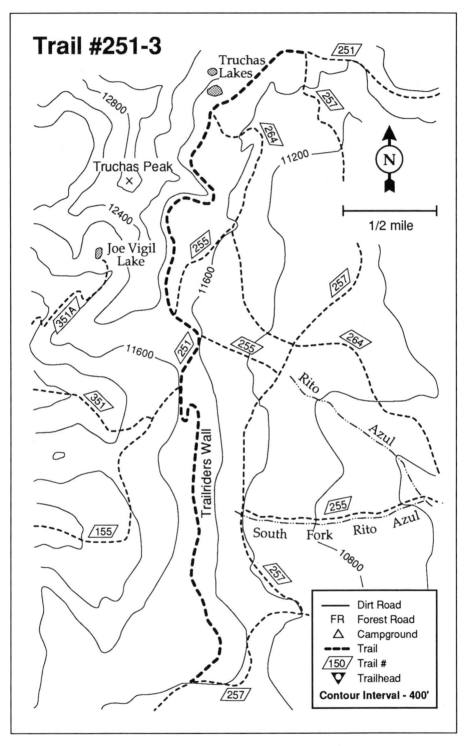

NOTE: contour intervals are at 400 feet

TRAIL 251, Part 3–SKYLINE TRAIL

LENGTH: 7 miles

RATING: Moderate

USE: Moderate

SEASONS: Early summer to late fall

HIGHEST & LOWEST POINTS: 11,920 ft. & 11,600 ft.

NOTES: Trailriders Wall is a high, open ridge and is not safe during a thunderstorm. Do not hike on the wall if a storm is approaching. *All lake basins in the wilderness are closed to camping and campfires.* These areas have been damaged by overuse. *Do not feed the sheep or any other wild animals.* Bighorn sheep in the area will not hesitate to enter camp-sites and get into unattended supplies. Keep food out of reach.

LOCATION: Pecos/Las Vegas Ranger District, Santa Fe National Forest

TRAIL ACCESS: Trail 257, south & north sections

USGS MAP: Truchas Peak

DESCRIPTION: Skyline Trail continues north from Trail 257 and ascends the long, wide, barren ridge between Pecos Baldy and Truchas Peaks known as Trailriders Wall. The trail follows the top of the wall for 2½ miles before beginning a gradual descent near the junction of Trail 155. The trail continues north through spruce forest past two obscure junctions with Trail 255, skirting the bases of the Truchas Peaks. South Truchas Peak, at 13,103 ft., is the second highest peak in New Mexico. The trail takes a short, steep climb up a hillside, passes Truchas Lakes, and con-tinues another mile to the north junction with Trail 257. The views are spectacular in all directions.

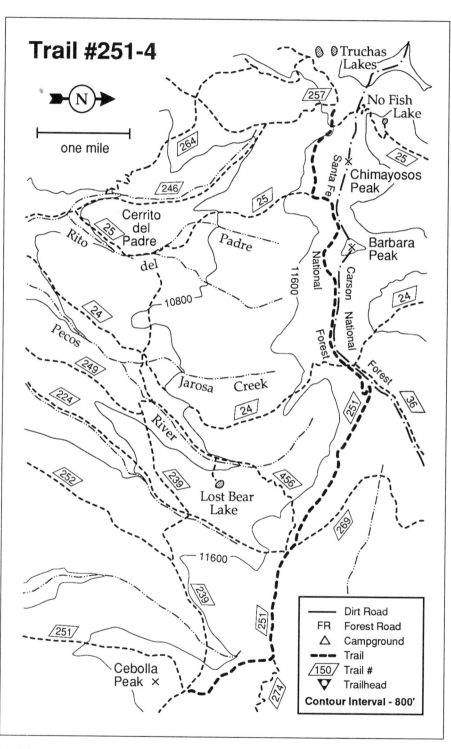

NOTE: contour intervals are at 800 feet

TRAIL 251, Part 4–SKYLINE TRAIL

LENGTH: 10 miles

RATING: Moderate

USE: Moderate

SEASONS: Summer to late fall

HIGHEST & LOWEST POINTS: 12,400 ft. & 11,800 ft.

NOTES: The Santa Barbara Divide is a high, open ridge and is not safe during thunderstorms. Do not hike on the divide if storm is approaching. *All lake basins in the wilderness are closed to camping and campfires.* These areas have been damaged by overuse. *Please do not feed the bighorn sheep or any other wild animals.*

LOCATION: Pecos/Las Vegas Ranger District, Santa Fe National Forest

TRAIL ACCESS: Trails 257 & 239

USGS MAPS: Pecos Falls, Truchas Peak, Gascon

DESCRIPTION: This section of Trail 251 is well fitted to the name of Skyline Trail as it crosses the entire length of the Santa Barbara Divide. From Trail 257, this trail continues east toward the divide. The traveler will come to two intersections with Trail 25 in the first 2 miles, traverse the south face of Chimayosos Peak, and emerge at the top of the divide. The trail continues east along the divide, passing Barbara Peak. Another 2 miles will find you at the junction with Trails 24 and 36. The trail traverses minor rises along the ridge and soon overlooks the Rincon Bonito valley. A mile south of this point is the junction of Trails 251, 269, 456, and 224. Trail 251 drops off the slope and turns east, passing through forest and emerging into a wide meadow. Continue east, looking for posts and cairns to orient travel. At the junction with Trail 274, continue across the meadow, then pass through forest and another large meadow. Continue southeast following cairns and posts to the edge of the divide. At this point, turn south along what is now the eastern divide and proceed along the edge of the ridge toward the grassy mound of Cebolla Peak and Trail 239. Due to light use, this last section of trail may be difficult to find and follow.

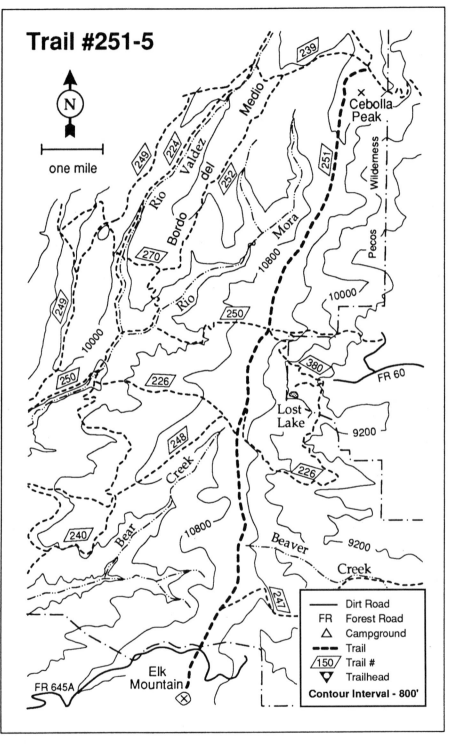

NOTE: contour intervals are at 800 feet

TRAIL 251, Part 5–SKYLINE TRAIL

LENGTH: 14½ miles

RATING: Moderate to difficult

USE: Light

SEASONS: Summer to early fall

HIGHEST & LOWEST POINTS: 11,800 ft. & 11,200 ft.

NOTES: The trail may be difficult to follow in the open meadows and is faint in some wooded sections. ***Avoid high points and open areas during thunderstorms.***

LOCATION: Pecos/Las Vegas Ranger District, Santa Fe National Forest

TRAIL ACCESS: Trail 239 & Forest Road 645A

USGS MAPS: Pecos Falls, Gascon, Elk Mountain

DESCRIPTION: This last section of Skyline Trail is more remote and less traveled than the other sections. From the junction with Trail 239, Trail 251 continues south along the eastern divide and skirts the west slope of Cebolla Peak. From here the trail alternates between meadows, boulder fields, and forested areas. After 6 miles the intersection with Trail 250 is encountered. From this point Skyline Trail continues south along the divide, traversing occasional small meadows. The intersection with Trail 226 is another 2 miles. 251 continues south across rocky alpine meadows and back into the conifer forests of the divide for 5 miles to the junction with Trail 247. Another 1½ miles brings you to FR 645A. The trail crosses the road and can be followed south along the ridge all the way to the summit of Elk Mountain and beyond.

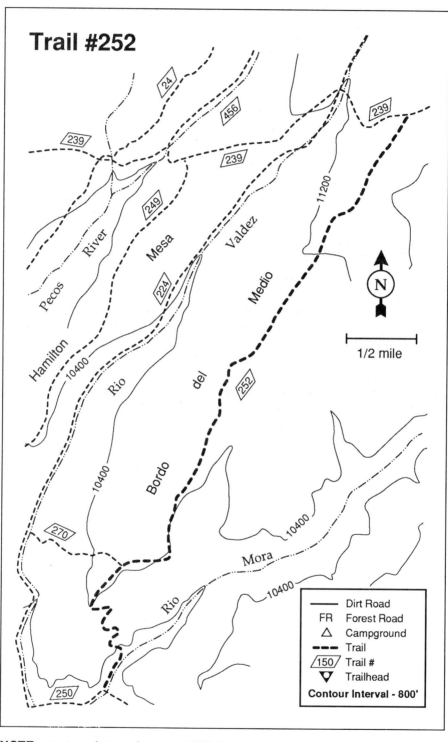

NOTE: contour intervals are at 800 feet

TRAIL 252–BORDO DEL MEDIO TRAIL

LENGTH: 7 miles

RATING: Moderate

USE: Light

SEASONS: Late spring to mid-fall

HIGHEST & LOWEST POINTS: 11,500 ft. & 9,000 ft.

NOTES: Do not camp next to springs along the trail. This will avoid disturbing wildlife dependent on the water source and will help preserve the natural beauty of the area. Heavy tree fall on this trail makes travel difficult for livestock.

LOCATION: Pecos/Las Vegas Ranger District, Santa Fe National Forest

TRAIL ACCESS: Trails 250 & 239

USGS MAPS: Pecos Falls, Elk Mountain

DESCRIPTION: Trail 252 runs down the middle of the ridge which lies between Hamilton Mesa on the west and the eastern divide on the east. From the junction with Trail 250 the trail immediately crosses to the north side of the Rio Mora, and follows the river upstream for about ½ mile. It then turns north and begins the steep, rocky ascent to the top of the Bordo del Medio. You will encounter the hard-to-find junction with Trail 270 at the top of the ridge. 252 curves around to the east side of the ridge and goes through forested areas and small meadows. Conifers growing close to the trail may create a narrow passage. The last mile of the trail crosses a large meadow with excellent views of the surrounding country. At the north end of the meadow the trail returns to mixed forest and connects with Trail 239.

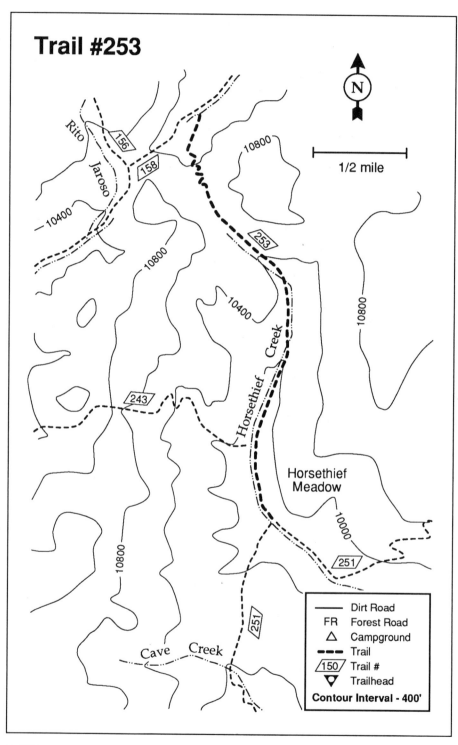

NOTE: contour intervals are at 400 feet

TRAIL 253

LENGTH: 3½ miles

RATING: Moderate

USE: Light

SEASONS: Late spring to mid-fall

HIGHEST & LOWEST POINTS: 10,640 ft. & 9,800 ft.

NOTES: This is a lightly traveled trail taking the visitor to a more remote area of the wilderness. A good trail for those seeking solitude.

LOCATION: Española and Pecos/Las Vegas ranger districts, Santa Fe National Forest

TRAIL ACCESS: Trails 251 & 158

USGS MAPS: Truchas Peak

DESCRIPTION: The trail may be difficult to find at its junction with Trail 251 near Horsethief Creek, but can be picked up in the treeline just north of the creek. From 251, go north across Horsethief Creek and follow Trail 253 until it turns northwest. The trail remains along the bank of the creek for about ½ mile before beginning the ascent to the top of a ridge. On the other side of the ridge the trail descends to the northwest into a side canyon by a series of switchbacks. Soon after a creek is reached, the intersection with Trail 158 is encountered. 253 ends here and the traveler can continue north or south along Trail 158.

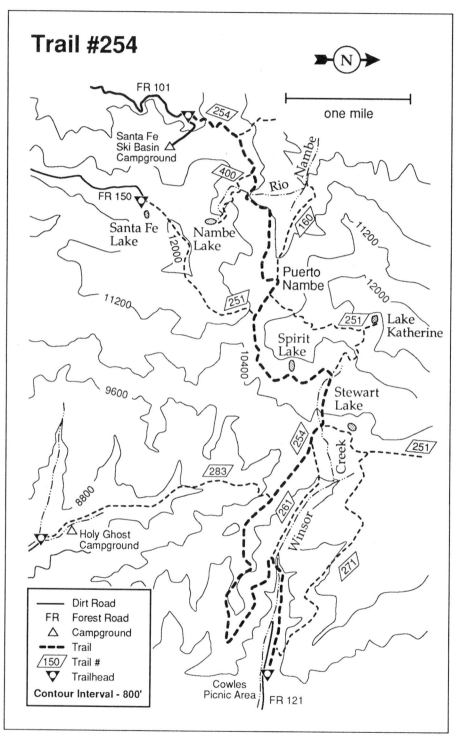

Trail #254

N

one mile

FR 101

Santa Fe
Ski Basin
Campground

254

400

FR 150

Santa Fe
Lake

Rio

Nambe

Nambe
Lake

12000

160

11200

Puerto
Nambe

12000

11200

251

251

Lake
Katherine

Spirit
Lake

10400

9600

Stewart
Lake

254

251

283

261

Winsor

Creek

8800

Holy Ghost
Campground

271

	Dirt Road
FR	Forest Road
△	Campground
- - -	Trail
150	Trail #
▽	Trailhead
Contour Interval - 800'	

Cowles
Picnic Area

FR 121

NOTE: contour intervals are at 800 feet

TRAIL 254–WINSOR TRAIL

LENGTH: 14 miles

RATING: Moderate

USE: Heavy

SEASONS: Late spring to mid-fall

HIGHEST & LOWEST POINTS: 10,800 ft. & 8,400 ft.

NOTES: **This is one of the most heavily used trails in the Pecos Wilderness.** The section of trail from Santa Fe Ski Basin Trailhead (described in Western Section Trailheads) to Puerto Nambe is especially well traveled. This is not the trail to take if the hiker is seeking solitude. The junction with Trail 283 is obscure. *All lake basins are closed to camping and campfires.* Overuse has caused severe resource damage in these areas. There are several good camping areas in the vicinity of Spirit and Stewart lakes that provide good campsites.

LOCATION: Española and Pecos/Las Vegas ranger districts, Santa Fe National Forest

TRAIL ACCESS: Santa Fe Ski Basin Trailhead & Cowles Trailhead

USGS MAPS: Aspen Basin, Cowles

DESCRIPTION: The trailhead at Santa Fe Ski Basin is easy to find and parking is ample. Trail 254 is found at the far north end of the parking lot. The first ½ mile of 254 switchbacks up to the top of a ridge and then descends through forest toward the Rio Nambe. After several stream crossings, you climb 200 feet to the grassy plateau known as Puerto Nambe and the junction with Trail 251 North. Continue east on 254. Another ½ mile brings you to the junction with Trail 251 South. Trail 254 descends through spruce forest for 1½ miles and passes by Spirit Lake. Another junction with Trail 251 lies 1 mile ahead. Continue east 1 mile on Trail 251/254 to the junction with Winsor Creek. 254 branches southeast and crosses the creek here. ½ mile east take the right fork again, avoiding the left fork which is old Trail 261, no longer maintained. Trail 254 continues southeast, passing through forested areas and large meadows and skirting Carpenter Ridge. This ridge has a southerly exposure and is hot and dry. The trail turns west on the north side of the ridge and descends through pine forests to Winsor Creek. Follow Winsor Creek, crossing several boggy areas before reaching the trailhead. This last section of 254 is lightly traveled.

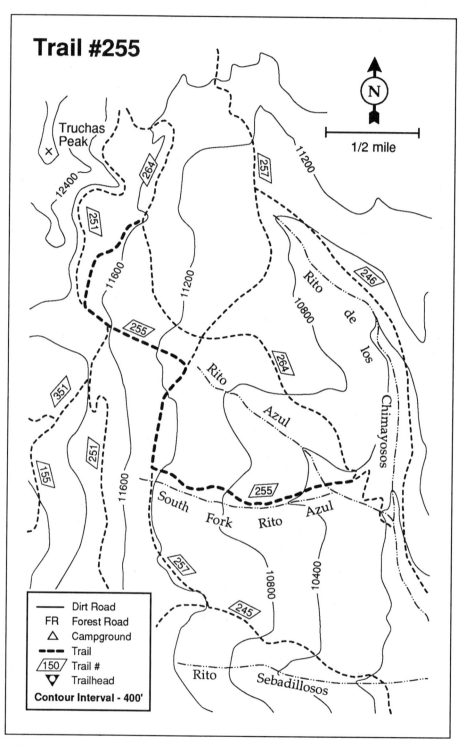

NOTE: contour intervals are at 400 feet

TRAIL 255–SOUTH AZUL TRAIL

LENGTH: 5 miles

RATING: Difficult

USE: Light

SEASONS: Mid-summer to mid-fall

HIGHEST & LOWEST POINTS: 11,840 ft. & 10,320 ft.

NOTES: This trail has not been maintained and significant tree fall may be encountered. The trail is also difficult to find and follow through the intermittent meadows. Many trail intersections are unmarked and are difficult to find. Well-traveled hunter trails make following the main trail very difficult. Sections of the trail are steep and severely eroded. The trail is not in the location shown on the Forest Service wilderness map. The trail stays on the north side of the South Fork Rito Azul for its entire length. The junctions are correct; the trail location is correct on the map in this guide. *All lake basins in the wilderness are closed to camping and campfires.*

LOCATION: Pecos/Las Vegas Ranger District, Santa Fe National Forest

TRAIL ACCESS: Trail 264, south & north segments

USGS MAPS: Pecos Falls, Truchas Peak

DESCRIPTION: From the southern section of Trail 264, Trail 255 heads almost due west across a meadow above the Rito Azul. After crossing the Azul, the trail travels through dense forest and occasional large meadows along the north side of the south fork of the Rito Azul. The junction with Trail 257 is located near the base of Trailriders Wall. Continue north on 255/257 until 255 turns to the northwest up the hillside just before a small stream crossing. This junction is very obscure. The trail continues northwest to its junction with Trail 251 and then turns north for ¾ mile to its terminus at the northern junction with 264. This last section of trail is very eroded and not recommended for livestock.

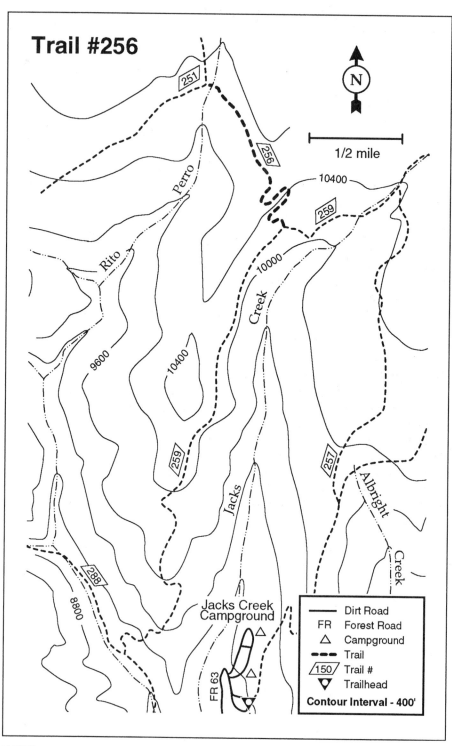

NOTE: contour intervals are at 400 feet

TRAIL 256–RITO PERRO TRAIL

LENGTH: 1½ miles

RATING: Moderate

USE: Moderate

SEASONS: Summer to fall

NOTES: The junction with Trail 259 may be difficult to find. Trail is hard to find in meadows.

LOCATION: Pecos/Las Vegas Ranger District, Santa Fe National Forest

TRAIL ACCESS: Trails 259 & 251

USGS MAP: Truchas Peak

DESCRIPTION: From the junction with Trail 259, Trail 256 travels northwest across the meadow, enters the trees, and begins to climb up a ridge on a series of switchbacks. The trail travels through mixed conifer forest and drops down into the Rito Perro drainage. This last ½ mile is very steep and rocky. The trail then crosses the Rito Perro, takes another short, steep climb out of the drainage, and ends at the junction with Trail 251.

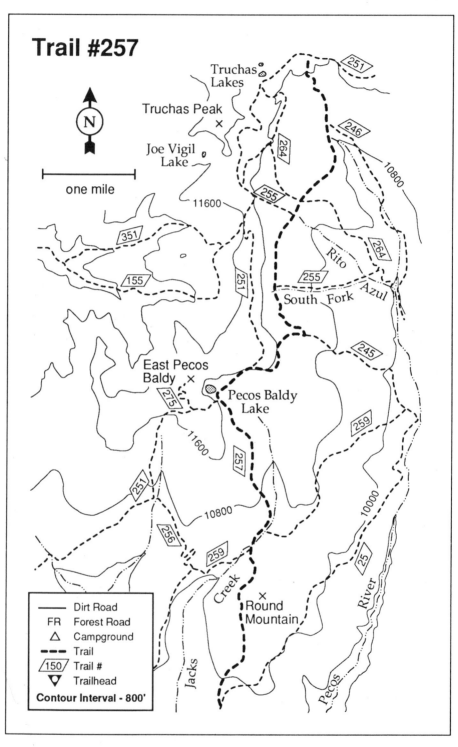

NOTE: contour intervals are at 800 feet

TRAIL 257–JACKS CREEK TRAIL

LENGTH: 14½ miles

RATING: Moderate

USE: Heavy

SEASONS: Early summer to mid-fall

HIGHEST & LOWEST POINTS: 11,840 ft. & 9,840 ft.

NOTES: All lake basins in the wilderness are closed to camping and camp-fires. Overuse has caused severe resource damage in these areas. *Do not feed the bighorn sheep or any other wild animals. The first 8 miles of this trail receive extremely heavy use.* People looking for solitude should hike or ride another trail.

LOCATION: Pecos/Las Vegas Ranger District, Santa Fe National Forest

TRAIL ACCESS: Trails 25 & 251

USGS MAPS: Cowles, Truchas Peak, Pecos Falls

DESCRIPTION: From Trail 25, Trail 257 heads north across the wide meadow circling Round Mountain. This is a popular area for cattle; expect to see them grazing here. The trail continues on a flat grade past Round Mountain to the Jacks Creek crossing and the junction with Trail 259. A moderate 3-mile climb through heavily wooded areas takes the traveler from Jacks Creek to the Pecos Baldy Lake area and the junction with Trail 251. This section is very muddy and boggy during the summer rainy season. Continue northeast on 251 about ¾ of a mile to pick up Trail 257. The trail climbs the ridge above Sebadillosos drainage to the top of Trailriders Wall, the long, wide ridge between Pecos Baldy and the Truchas Peaks. The trail then heads north and east down the hillside to the junction with Trail 245 (this section can stay snow covered and icy till July and can be hazardous) and then follows along the base of Trail-riders Wall, traveling through spruce forests and small meadows. After 2 miles the trail crosses the head of the Rito Azul and the second inter-section with Trail 255. Another ¼ mile brings the hiker to the junction with Trail 264, found in a flat meadow. From this point Trail 257 continues north through the forest for a short distance and then swings east briefly to drop into the Chimayosos drainage. The trail again turns to the north-west and follows the drainage up to the head of the canyon. Tree fall and boggy or marshy areas may slow travel considerably. The turnoff to Chimayosos Trail (246) is inconspicuous and may go unnoticed. At the head of the canyon, Trail 257 climbs quickly through meadows to the northern junction with Trail 251.

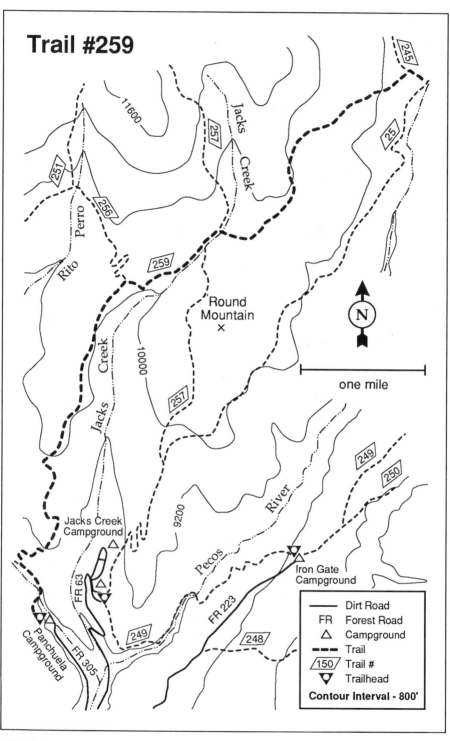

Trail #259

NOTE: contour intervals are at 800 feet

TRAIL 259–DOCKWILLER TRAIL

LENGTH: 9 miles

RATING: Difficult

USE: Moderate

SEASONS: Late spring to early fall

HIGHEST & LOWEST POINTS: 10,800 ft. & 8,300 ft.

NOTES: All lake basins in the wilderness are closed to camping and camp-fires. The Beattys Flats area is closed to camping and campfires. Overuse has caused severe resource damage in these areas. See closure map for exact boundaries of closure area.

LOCATION: Pecos/Las Vegas Ranger District, Santa Fe National Forest

TRAIL ACCESS: Panchuela Trailhead & Trail 25

USGS MAPS: Cowles, Pecos Falls, Truchas Peak

DESCRIPTION: This trail offers a less traveled route to the central Pecos. From the parking area, walk north through the campground and cross the bridge over Panchuela Creek. Follow the trail for about 1 mile and look for the turnoff to the north. At this point, Trail 288 goes northwest up the creek and Trail 259 begins a steep climb up several switchbacks through pine forests to the top of a ridge. The trail levels off considerably but still continues to climb through aspen groves to the junction with Trail 256. These aspen groves are a colorful sight in the fall. Trail 259 continues to the east along the slope of the Jacks Creek drainage and merges with Trail 257 after about a mile. At this junction the visitor continues up 257 about ¼ mile for the turnoff and continuation of Trail 259. At the turnoff, there is a well-worn trail that goes north up Jacks Creek. This is Trail 257, not 259. Trail 259 crosses Jacks Creek and heads east up the hillside. The trail climbs through large open meadows and forest for about 2 miles before beginning a steep descent into the upper meadows above Beattys Flats. The junction with Trail 245 is encountered in the last ¼ mile before this trail's terminus at Trail 25.

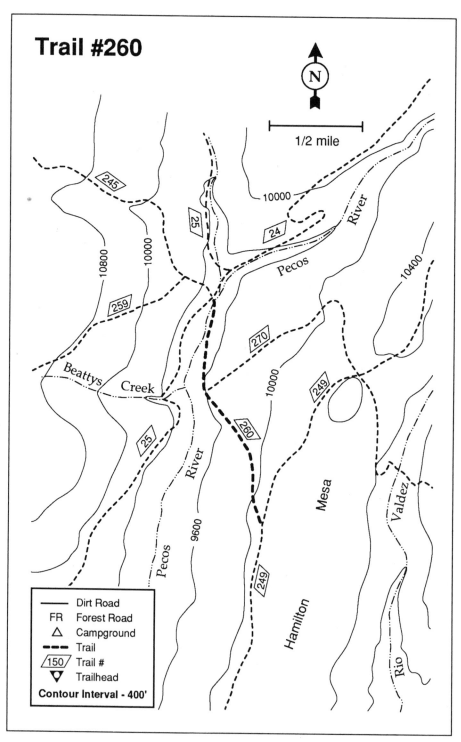

Trail #260

N

1/2 mile

Contour Interval - 400'

——	Dirt Road
FR	Forest Road
△	Campground
- - -	Trail
150	Trail #
▽	Trailhead

NOTE: contour intervals are at 400 feet

TRAIL 260–LARKSPUR TRAIL

LENGTH: 2 miles

RATING: Easy

USE: Heavy

SEASONS: Summer to mid-fall

HIGHEST & LOWEST POINTS: 10,080 ft. & 9,360 ft.

NOTES: This is a heavily used and popular trail. The Beattys Flats area is closed to camping and campfires. Overuse has caused severe resource damage. See closure map for exact boundaries of the closure area.

LOCATION: Pecos/Las Vegas Ranger District, Santa Fe National Forest

TRAIL ACCESS: Trails 249 & 25

USGS MAPS: Pecos Falls, Elk Mountain

DESCRIPTION: From Trail 249, Trail 260 heads northwest across Hamilton Mesa and makes a gradual descent into the Pecos River valley over the next 1½ miles. The trail alternates between open meadows, conifers, and aspen forests. At the intersection with the Pecos River, a well-constructed footbridge offers an easy crossing to the west bank of the river and the open, grassy valley of Beattys Flats. This trail gets very muddy and boggy in the rainy season.

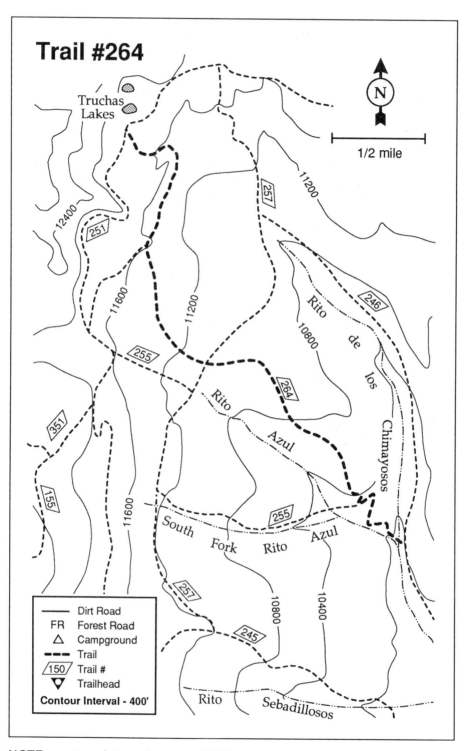

Trail #264

Truchas Lakes

N

1/2 mile

12400

251

11200

257

11200

11600

11200

255

Rito de los Chimayosos

246

10800

264

351

Rito

155

Azul

11600

255

South Fork Rito Azul

257

10800

10400

245

Rito Sebadillosos

——	Dirt Road
FR	Forest Road
△	Campground
- - -	Trail
150	Trail #
▽	Trailhead
Contour Interval - 400'	

NOTE: contour intervals are at 400 feet

TRAIL 264–NORTH AZUL TRAIL

LENGTH: 4 miles

RATING: Moderate

USE: Light

SEASONS: Summer to mid-fall

HIGHEST & LOWEST POINTS: 11,760 ft. & 10,000 ft.

*NOTES: **All lake basins in the wilderness are closed to camping and camp-fires.*** Overuse has caused severe resource damage in this area.

LOCATION: Pecos/Las Vegas Ranger District, Santa Fe National Forest

TRAIL ACCESS: Trails 246 & 251

USGS MAPS: Pecos Falls, Truchas Peak

DESCRIPTION: At the intersection of Trails 264 and 246 the hiker must cross to the west side of the Rito de los Chimayosos. The trail immediately begins a steep climb out of the canyon and follows a ridge between the Chimayosos and the Rito Azul. After 1½ miles of climbing, the trail enters a large meadow and intersects with Trail 257. Trail 264 continues northwest and climbs with an easier grade for another mile. The trail turns more to the north, traversing minor ridges fingering out from the main slope of the Truchas Peaks for another mile. The trail again climbs abruptly up the slope to emerge at a large, boggy meadow, skirts the bog along the northwest side, and again climbs steeply up the hillside in the final ascent to the open areas at the junction with Trail 251, ¼ mile south of Truchas Lakes.

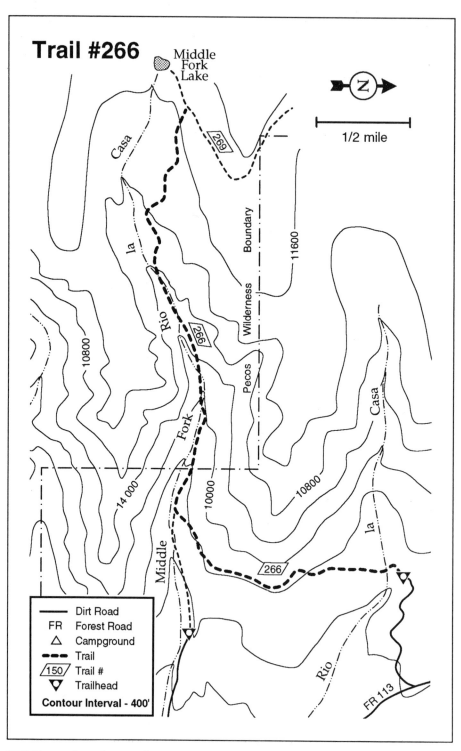

NOTE: contour intervals are at 400 feet

TRAIL 266

LENGTH: 5 miles

RATING: Moderate

USE: Light

SEASONS: Summer to fall

NOTES: ***All lake basins are closed to camping and campfires due to resource damage.*** Trailhead is difficult to find. Trail location is not shown correctly on Forest Service wilderness map.

LOCATION: Pecos/Las Vegas Ranger District, Santa Fe National Forest

TRAIL ACCESS: Forest Road 113 & Trail 269

USGS MAPS: Gascon, Pecos Falls

DESCRIPTION: From the trailhead, Trail 266 heads south, then turns southwest when it gets near the private land. The trail soon begins a steep, rocky ascent up the middle fork of the Rio la Casa. This section of trail is difficult to hike or ride, but the many small waterfalls are scenic attractions. After about 2½ miles, the trail breaks away from the stream bed, continuing to travel through mixed conifer forest. The trail ends at the junction with Trail 269.

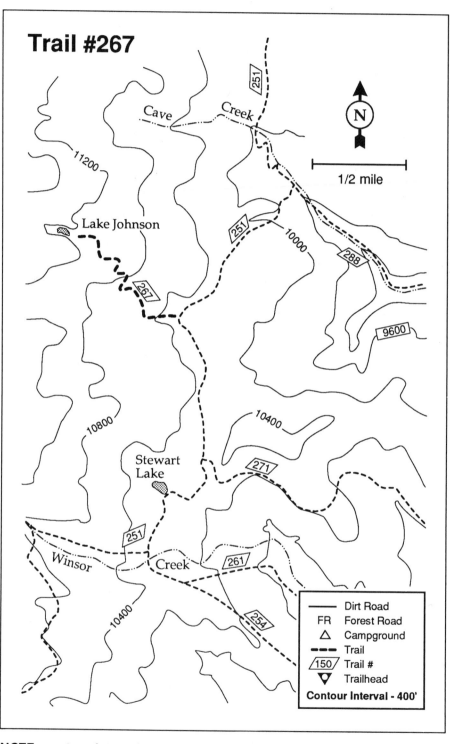

Trail #267

NOTE: contour intervals are at 400 feet

TRAIL 267–LAKE JOHNSON TRAIL

LENGTH: 1¾ miles

RATING: Moderate

USE: Light

SEASONS: Summer through fall

HIGHEST & LOWEST POINTS: 11,200 ft. & 10,400 ft.

NOTES: **All lake basins are closed to camping and campfires.** Overuse has caused severe resource damage in this area.

LOCATION: Pecos/Las Vegas Ranger District, Santa Fe National Forest

TRAIL ACCESS: Trail 251

USGS MAP: Cowles

DESCRIPTION: From Trail 251, about 150 yards north of the Rito Oscuro, Trail 267 skirts the northern boundary of a large, boggy meadow. From here the hiker will travel up the hillside, remaining considerably north of the stream. The incline is steady but fairly steep as the trail climbs almost 700 ft. to the lake basin nestled just below Redondo Peak.

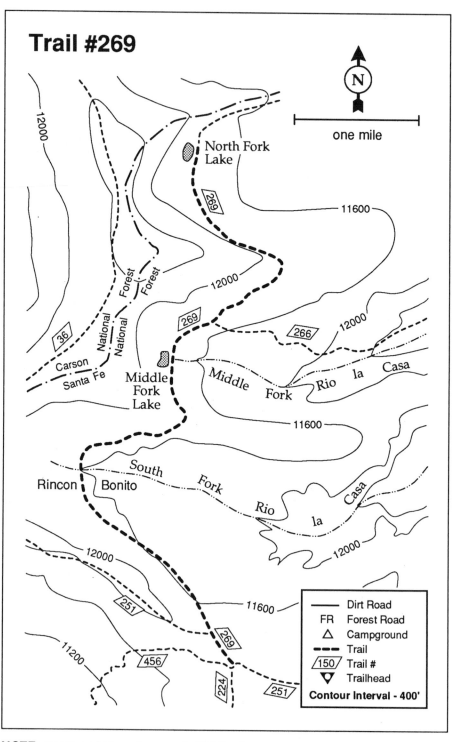

Trail #269

N one mile

North Fork Lake

269

11600

12000

Forest Forest

National National

36

Carson

Santa Fe

12000

269

266

12000

Middle Fork Lake

Middle Fork Rio la Casa

11600

South Fork

Rincon Bonito

Rio la Casa

12000

12000

251

11600

269

11200

456

224

251

	Dirt Road
FR	Forest Road
△	Campground
---	Trail
150	Trail #
▽	Trailhead
Contour Interval - 400'	

NOTE: contour intervals are at 400 feet

TRAIL 269–NORTH FORK TRAIL

LENGTH: 4½ miles

RATING: Easy

USE: Moderate

SEASONS: Summer to early fall

HIGHEST & LOWEST POINTS: 11,800 ft. & 11,600 ft.

*NOTES: **All lake basins are closed to camping and campfires.*** Overuse of these areas has caused severe resource damage.

LOCATION: Pecos/Las Vegas Ranger District, Santa Fe National Forest

TRAIL ACCESS: Trail 251

USGS MAPS: Jicarita Peak, Pecos Falls

DESCRIPTION: This is one of the more primitive and scenic areas in the Pecos Wilderness. Trail 269 is accessible at its northern end from Forest Road 113. It is a hike of approximately 4 miles from FR 113 to North Fork Lake. From North Fork Lake the trail follows along the base of the Jicarita Peak ridge. This area is wet and marshy, collecting the drainage off this ridge and forming the headwaters of the Rio la Casa. At 2 miles, Middle Fork Lake is encountered. From here the trail curves around an outcropping of the Jicarita ridge and enters the Rincon Bonito area. Surrounded by the Santa Barbara Divide and the Jicarita ridge, the Rincon Bonito forms a protected valley with lush meadows interspersed with willow and conifer forests. From here the trail climbs about 200 ft. in 1½ miles to the top of the Santa Barbara Divide and the intersection with Trail 251. Beautiful views of the surrounding area can be seen from here.

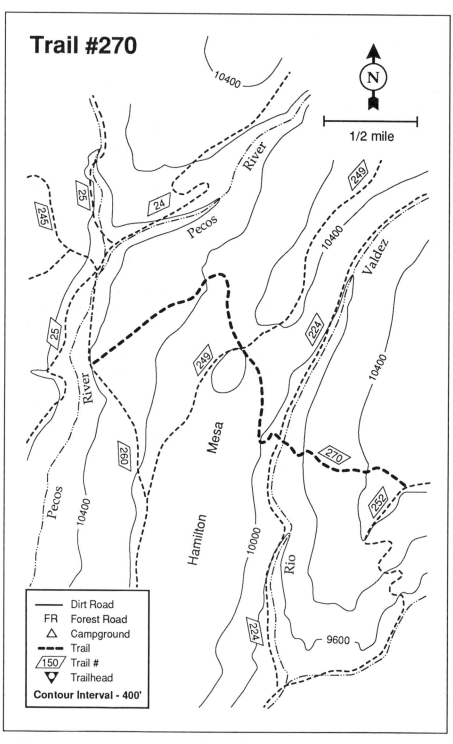

NOTE: contour intervals are at 400 feet

TRAIL 270–BOB GROUNDS TRAIL

LENGTH: 4 miles

RATING: Moderate

USE: Moderate

SEASONS: Summer through fall

HIGHEST & LOWEST POINTS: 10,400 ft. & 9,600 ft.

NOTES: This is one of the lesser traveled trails from the Beattys Flats area. Several sections are extremely steep, eroded, and rocky. Numerous cow trails in the meadows can make sections of Trail 270 difficult to locate.

LOCATION: Pecos/Las Vegas Ranger District, Santa Fe National Forest

TRAIL ACCESS: Trails 260 & 252

USGS MAP: Pecos Falls

DESCRIPTION: From Trail 260, this trail travels through dense forest for ½ mile before emerging into several small meadows. At the top of Hamilton Mesa, the traveler will encounter Trail 249 heading south and shortly thereafter Trail 249 heading north. Trail 270 continues southeast along a small drainage and drops steeply down the hillside to the Rio Valdez. This is the steepest section of the trail and is severely eroded in sections. Upon reaching the Rio Valdez, one must proceed upstream about ¼ mile to locate the remaining section of Trail 270 up the Bordo del Medio ridge. At this point the trail crosses to the east of the Rio Valdez and begins a mile-long steep, rocky, eroded ascent up the ridge to the trail's junction with Trail 252.

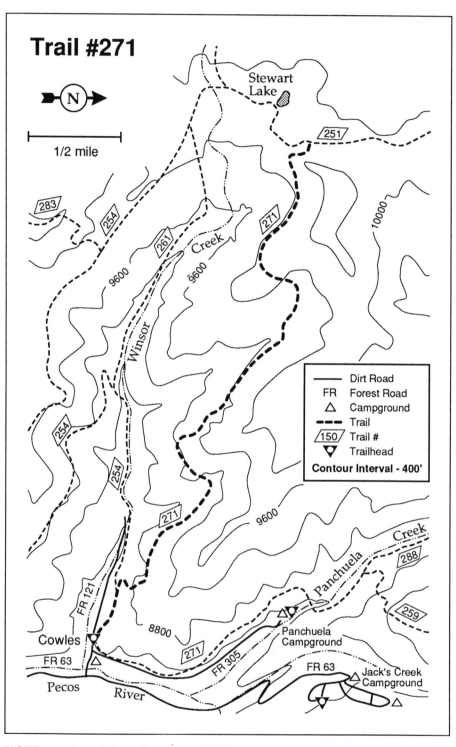

Trail #271

N

1/2 mile

Stewart Lake

251

283

254

261

Creek

271

10000

9600

9600

Winsor

254

254

271

9600

Panchuela Creek

288

259

FR 121

271

8800

Panchuela Campground

Cowles

FR 63

271

FR 305

FR 63

Jack's Creek Campground

Pecos River

Dirt Road
FR Forest Road
△ Campground
- - - Trail
150 Trail #
▽ Trailhead
Contour Interval - 400'

NOTE: contour intervals are at 400 feet

TRAIL 271–WINSOR RIDGE TRAIL

LENGTH: 6 miles

RATING: Moderate

USE: Moderate

SEASONS: Summer through fall

HIGHEST & LOWEST POINTS: 10,200 ft. & 8,300 ft.

*NOTES: **All lake basins in the wilderness are closed to camping and camp-fires.*** Overuse has caused severe resource damage in this area.

LOCATION: Pecos/Las Vegas Ranger District, Santa Fe National Forest

TRAIL ACCESS: Cowles Trailhead & Trail 251

USGS MAP: Cowles

DESCRIPTION: This trail offers easy access from the Pecos canyon to the west side of the wilderness. The trail begins in a small meadow near the Cowles parking area, climbs up the hillside, and heads west above the summer home area along Forest Road 121. Open meadows alternate with scrub oak, aspen, and conifers as the trail climbs steadily up the hillside. Openings give the traveler views of the surrounding country. This is a beautiful sight in the fall, when the colors of the oak and aspen mix with the green of the conifers. The trail remains on the south face of the hillside just below the ridgetop north of Winsor Creek, passing through aspen groves and skirting meadows. The last mile of trail passes through mixed conifer forest. Trail 271 levels off at the top of the ridge just before the intersection with Trail 251.

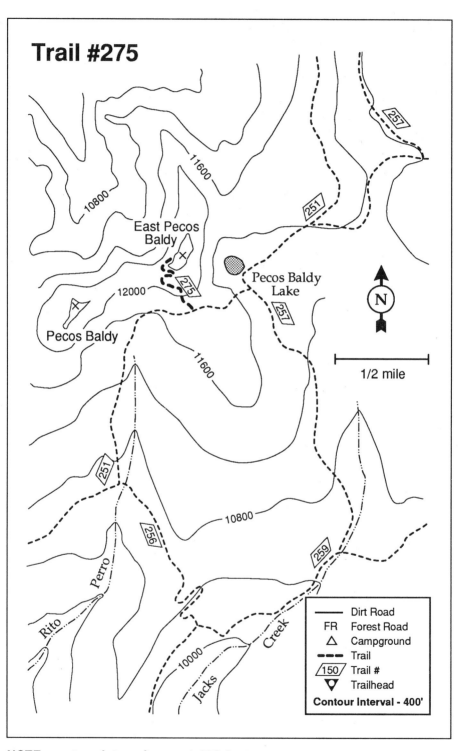

Trail #275

10800
11600
257
251
East Pecos Baldy
12000
275
Pecos Baldy
Pecos Baldy Lake
257
11600
N
1/2 mile
251
256
10800
259
Perro
Rito
Creek
10000
Jacks

	Dirt Road
FR	Forest Road
△	Campground
---	Trail
150	Trail #
▽	Trailhead
Contour Interval - 400'	

NOTE: contour intervals are at 400 feet

TRAIL 275–EAST PECOS BALDY TRAIL

LENGTH: 1 mile round-trip

RATING: Difficult

USE: Moderate

SEASONS: Mid-summer to mid-fall

HIGHEST & LOWEST POINTS: 12,530 ft. & 11,975 ft.

NOTES: All lake basins in the wilderness are closed to camping and campfires. Do not feed the bighorn sheep or any other wild animals.

LOCATION: Pecos/Las Vegas Ranger District, Santa Fe National Forest

TRAIL ACCESS: Trail 251

USGS MAP: Truchas Peak

DESCRIPTION: The trail takes off from Trail 251 at the saddle on Pecos Baldy Lake ridge and switchbacks up the south and southeast face of East Pecos Baldy. The climb is steep, the trail is rocky, and the high altitude adds to the difficulty of the trip for the hiker. Be alert for the signs of altitude sickness. *Allow at least three hours for the round trip and be prepared to abandon the ascent at the first sign of inclement weather.*

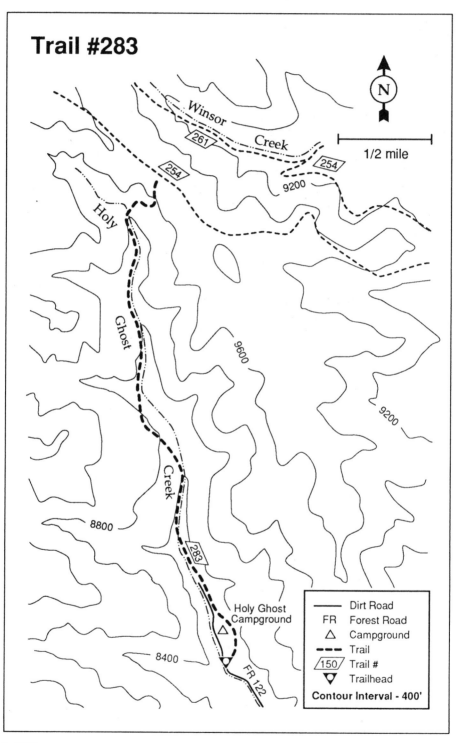

Trail #283

NOTE: contour intervals are at 400 feet

TRAIL 283–HOLY GHOST TRAIL

LENGTH: 5 miles

RATING: Moderate

USE: Moderate

SEASONS: Late spring to mid-fall

HIGHEST & LOWEST POINTS: 9,840 ft. & 8,160 ft.

NOTES: **All lake basins in the wilderness are closed to camping and camp-fires.** Overuse has caused severe resource damage in these areas. This is a popular trail for day hikers staying in the campground and receives heavy use on weekends.

LOCATION: Pecos/Las Vegas Ranger District, Santa Fe National Forest

TRAIL ACCESS: Holy Ghost Trailhead & Trail 254

USGS MAP: Cowles

DESCRIPTION: The trail begins on the east side of the trailhead parking lot, climbing out of the canyon and curving along the pine-and-oak-covered hillside above the campground. The trail drops back down to Holy Ghost Creek and follows it along the boggy, grassy creek bottom for ½ mile. It then begins another climb out of the canyon and into the forested hillsides. There are several easy stream crossings along the way. The trail is steep when climbing out of these crossings. The last mile of trail switchbacks up the slope and emerges in an open meadow along the ridge south of Winsor Creek. Please stay on the trail and avoid taking the shortcuts. These shortcuts are steep, eroded, and dangerous. The intersection with Trail 254 is encountered here, though the junction is vague. Trail 283 ends here while Trail 254 continues northwest and southeast.

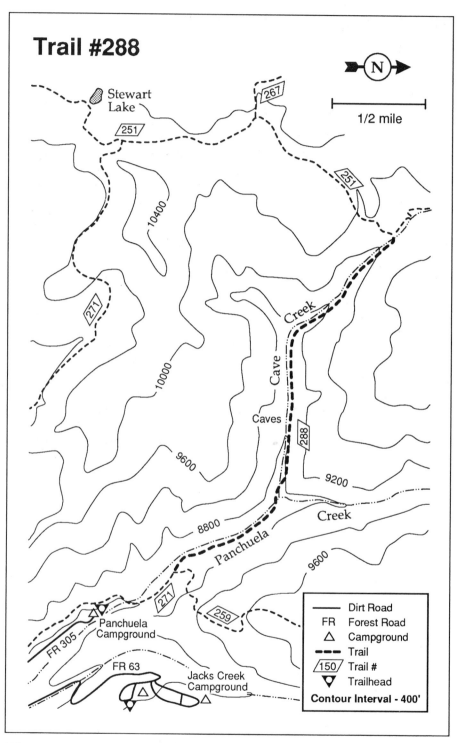

Trail #288

N

1/2 mile

Stewart Lake

251

267

251

271

10400

10000

Cave Creek

Caves

288

9600

9200

8800

Creek

Panchuela

9600

271

259

Panchuela Campground

FR 305

FR 63

Jacks Creek Campground

	Dirt Road
FR	Forest Road
△	Campground
- - -	Trail
150	Trail #
▽	Trailhead
Contour Interval - 400'	

NOTE: contour intervals are at 400 feet

TRAIL 288–CAVE CREEK TRAIL

LENGTH: 5 miles

RATING: Moderate

USE: Heavy

SEASONS: Late spring through fall

HIGHEST & LOWEST POINTS: 9,720 ft. & 8,400 ft.

NOTES: All lake basins in the wilderness are closed to camping and campfires. Overuse has caused severe resource damage in this area. This trail is very popular with day hikers out of Panchuela Campground and receives very heavy use on weekends.

LOCATION: Pecos/Las Vegas Ranger District, Santa Fe National Forest

TRAIL ACCESS: Panchuela Trailhead & Trail 251

USGS MAP: Cowles

DESCRIPTION: From the parking area, walk through the campground, cross the bridge over Panchuela Creek, and follow the trail upstream. The turnoff to Trail 259 is encountered in the first mile. Trail 288 begins a gradual climb northwest to the junction of Panchuela Creek and Cave Creek. The trail crosses Panchuela Creek via a log bridge and continues along the north side of Cave Creek. (Some maps show the trail on the south side of the creek; this is incorrect.) After ½ mile the caves along Cave Creek can be found on the south side of the creek. The caves were formed by the creek flowing underground. This is a fragile area; please be careful when exploring. After passing the caves, Trail 288 continues up the canyon on the north bank of the creek, making a steep climb through aspen and conifer forests to the junction with Trail 251. This section of trail is also very eroded.

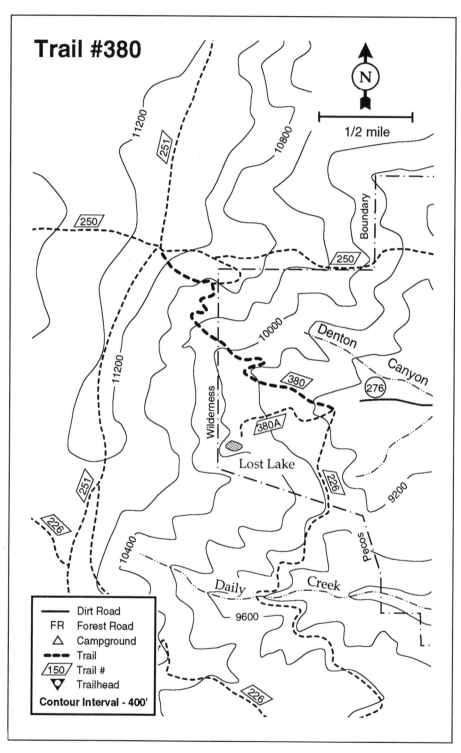

Trail #380

N

1/2 mile

11200
251
250
10800
Boundary
250
10000
Denton
Canyon
380
276
Wilderness
380A
Lost Lake
11200
226
9200
251
Pecos
226
10400
Daily Creek
9600
226

Dirt Road
FR Forest Road
△ Campground
- - - Trail
150 Trail #
▽ Trailhead
Contour Interval - 400'

NOTE: contour intervals are at 400 feet

TRAIL 380–MAESTAS TRAIL

LENGTH: 2½ miles

RATING: Difficult

USE: Light

SEASONS: Summer to fall

NOTES: **Not recommended.** Junctions are difficult to find. You must obtain permission from the owner of the private land to use the trail.

LOCATION: Pecos/Las Vegas Ranger District, Santa Fe National Forest

TRAIL ACCESS: State Highway 276 & Trails 250, 251

USGS MAPS: Rociada, Elk Mountain

DESCRIPTION: From your parking spot beside Highway 276, walk west along the road; 100 yards before it ends, turn left on a small dirt road crossing a stream. Follow this road to an old cabin, then follow the fencing found north of the cabin uphill and to the west until it makes a right-angle turn to the north. At this point, a trail continues along the fence down to another stream crossing. The trail then makes a sharp turn west at the back gate of the Martinez cabin. From here, the trail begins a steep and rocky ascent along the drainage of a tributary of the Maestas River. The trail turns northwest up a side canyon, traveling through the forest and then entering meadows as it nears the eastern divide. Gulleys and cow trails here make the junction with Trail 250 difficult to find, but wonderful views of the surrounding countryside reward the traveler at the divide.

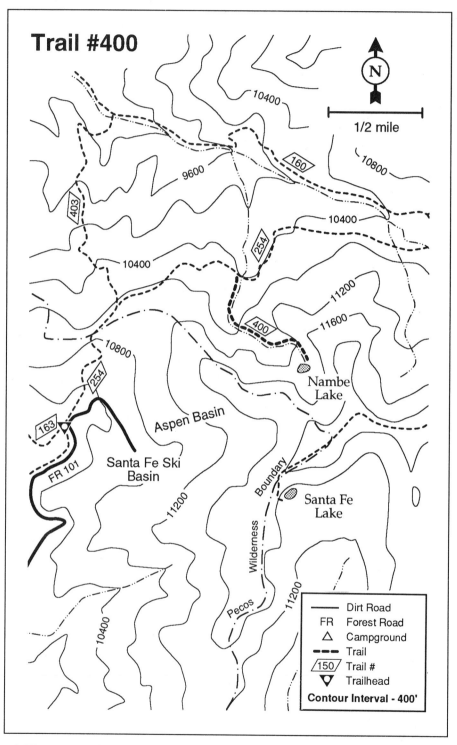

Trail #400

N

1/2 mile

10400

160

9600

403

10800

10400

254

10400

11200

400

11600

10800

254

Nambe Lake

163

Aspen Basin

Santa Fe Ski Basin

FR 101

11200

Boundary

Santa Fe Lake

Wilderness

Pecos

11200

10400

	Dirt Road
FR	Forest Road
△	Campground
- - -	Trail
150	Trail #
▽	Trailhead
Contour Interval - 400'	

NOTE: contour intervals are at 400 feet

TRAIL 400-NAMBE LAKE TRAIL

LENGTH: 1 mile

RATING: Difficult

USE: Moderate

SEASONS: Late summer to fall

NOTES: **All lake basins are closed to camping and campfires due to resource damage.** The trail is steep and rocky. It does not follow the route shown on Forest Service wilderness map, but goes straight up Nambe Lake Creek; trail is not shown on USGS maps.

LOCATION: Española Ranger District, Santa Fe National Forest

TRAIL ACCESS: Trail 254

USGS MAP: Aspen Basin

DESCRIPTION: The trail begins from 254 about 100 yards west of the Nambe Lake Creek crossing. The trail travels straight up the drainage to Nambe Lake, where it deadends. In many places there are several parallel trails all following various routes up the drainage.

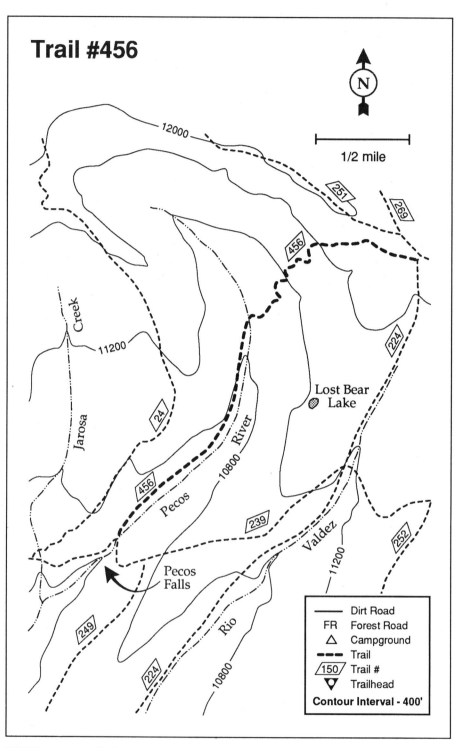

Trail #456

N

1/2 mile

12000

251

269

456

224

Creek

11200

Jarosa

24

Lost Bear Lake

456

River

10800

Pecos

239

Valdez

11200

252

Pecos Falls

249

Rio

224

10800

	Dirt Road
FR	Forest Road
△	Campground
---	Trail
150	Trail #
▽	Trailhead
Contour Interval - 400'	

NOTE: contour intervals are at 400 feet

TRAIL 456–PECOS RIVER TRAIL

LENGTH: 4 miles

RATING: Difficult

USE: Moderate

SEASONS: Summer to mid-fall

HIGHEST & LOWEST POINTS: 11,760 ft. & 10,660 ft.

NOTES: **The Pecos Falls area is closed to camping and campfires.** Overuse has caused severe resource damage in this area. See closure map for exact boundaries of closure area. There are several parallel trails along the river for the first 2 miles and this can be very confusing for the hiker. The trail along the bank of the river is intermittent and often dead ends in marshy bogs.

LOCATION: Pecos/Las Vegas Ranger District, Santa Fe National Forest

TRAIL ACCESS: Trails 239 & 251

USGS MAP: Pecos Falls

DESCRIPTION: This trail follows the Pecos River to its headwaters and then climbs the ridge to the Santa Barbara Divide. From Trail 239, pick up 456 just west of the Pecos River above Pecos Falls. Follow the trail along the higher slope and follow it upstream as it parallels the Pecos, remaining within ¼ mile of the river. After 2 miles, the trail crosses the river at a fence and begins a steep climb through forest and small meadows to the Santa Barbara Divide. This section of the trail is steep, rocky, and eroded. The trail may become vague but it continues to the east across the top of the saddle. The trail terminates in a large, open area at the junction with Trails 251, 269, and 224.

WESTERN SECTION
TRAILHEADS

Trailheads are not patrolled. Do not leave valuable items in your vehicle. Do not leave your vehicle parked unattended for extended periods of time. You may wish to arrange shuttles or drop-offs. If your vehicle is broken into or vandalized, notify the Forest Service and the county sheriff.

ASPEN VISTA and SANTA FE SKI BASIN: From Santa Fe, follow the signs to Hyde Park and the ski basin. Aspen Vista is a small parking and picnic area just 1½ miles south of Santa Fe Ski Basin. Forest Road 150, the long, winding dirt road to the top of Tesuque Peak and the start of Trail 251 is closed to motor vehicles. The trailhead to Trail 254 is located at the northwest end of the ski basin parking lot. *Access to Trails 251 and 254 (see Central Section); Trail 403 is nearby off 254.*

ASPEN RANCH: This is approached most easily from Forest Road 101 to Santa Fe Ski Basin. Just before Aspen Vista Campground, take a left turn on Forest Road 102 and follow the signs to Aspen Ranch. *Access to Trail 150.*

BORREGO MESA: Take State Highway 4 through Nambe and Cundiyo. About 2 miles north of Cundiyo look for Forest Road 306 to Borrego Campground. Camping and horse corrals are available. There is no camping fee. *Due to the remote location and the high incidence of vandalism here, visitors may wish to avoid overnight parking. Access to Trails 153 and 155; nearby are 150, 151, and 157.*

CUNDIYO: Closest access is from the town of Cundiyo on State Highway 4. A dirt road to the south about 1 mile west of Cundiyo will take you directly to the trailhead along the Rio Frijoles. However, this is private land and no parking areas are available. There is a gate across the access road. You will need landowner's permission to park. *This trailhead has a high incidence of vandalism. Access to Trail 154; western terminus of Trail 156.*

NAMBE RESERVOIR: Take State Highway 4 through Nambe Pueblo and follow the road to Nambe Reservoir. The trailhead can be picked up on the north side of the reservoir. A fee may be required for the use of the area. You will need permission from Nambe Pueblo to park at this trailhead. *Access to Trail 160 and from there to 158.*

The maps accompanying the trail descriptions are for orientation only. For a more detailed representation of topographic features, please refer to the wilderness map or appropriate USGS quadrangles.

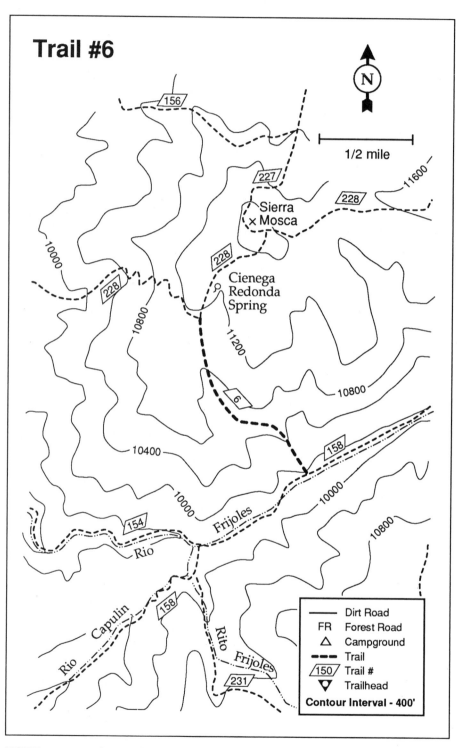

NOTE: contour intervals are at 400 feet

TRAIL 6

LENGTH: 2 miles

RATING: Difficult

USE: Light

SEASONS: Late spring to mid-fall

HIGHEST & LOWEST POINTS: 11,120 ft. & 9,920 ft.

*NOTES: **This trail is not recommended.*** This trail is extremely steep and can be hazardous to hikers and horses.

LOCATION: Española Ranger District, Santa Fe National Forest

TRAIL ACCESS: Trails 158 & 228

USGS MAP: Sierra Mosca

DESCRIPTION: From Trail 158 this trail begins the steep ascent out of the Frijoles drainage immediately and climbs to the top of a ridge within the first ¼ mile. From here the trail levels out slightly, but continues to climb along the side of a small drainage for another ½ mile. The terrain soon opens up into a large boggy meadow with the trail skirting up the northwest edge. Within another ¼ mile the trail opens up into the large meadows of Cienega Redonda and the junction with Trail 228.

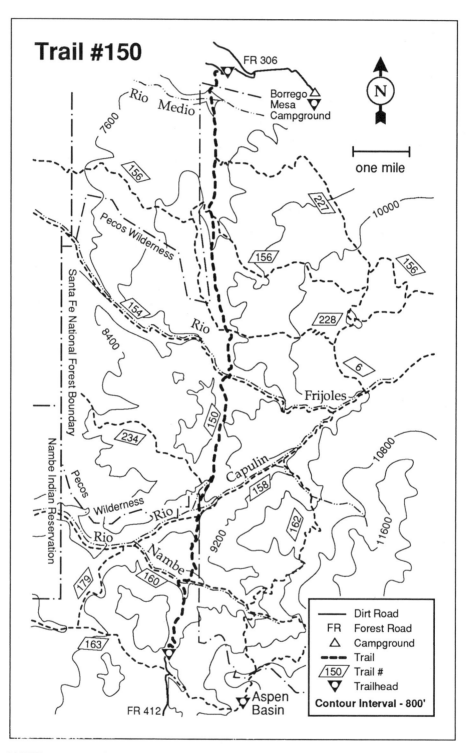

Trail #150

FR 306

Borrego
Mesa
Campground

N

one mile

Rio Medio

7600

10000

156

227

Pecos Wilderness

156

156

154

228

8400

Rio

6

Santa Fe National Forest Boundary

Frijoles

150

234

10800

Capulin

Nambe Indian Reservation

158

Pecos

162

Wilderness

Rio

11600

9200

Rio

Nambe

179

160

163

FR 412

Aspen
Basin

	Dirt Road
FR	Forest Road
△	Campground
- - -	Trail
150	Trail #
▽	Trailhead

Contour Interval - 800'

NOTE: contour intervals are at 800 feet

TRAIL 150–BORREGO TRAIL

LENGTH: 17 miles

RATING: Difficult

USE: Light

SEASONS: Late spring to mid-fall

HIGHEST & LOWEST POINTS: 9,200 ft. & 8,000 ft.

NOTES: This trail travels through rugged country and encounters very little level terrain. It is dry and warm, making this section available for travel almost a month earlier in the season than the rest of the wilderness.

LOCATION: Española Ranger District, Santa Fe National Forest

TRAIL ACCESS: Aspen Ranch & Borrego Mesa trailheads

USGS MAPS: Aspen Basin, Sierra Mosca

DESCRIPTION: From the meadows of Aspen Ranch, look for signs directing the visitor up a dirt road to the north. The trail begins ½ mile up this road. From here the trail begins a gradual descent down a side canyon to the Rio Nambe. After crossing to the north side of the river, proceed about ¼ mile up the canyon and look to the north for a signpost marking the continuation of the trail. The trail climbs over the ridge separating the Rio Capulin and Rio Nambe drainages, then drops down to Rancho Viejo, crosses to the north side of the Rio Capulin and heads up Cañada Vaca. The junction with Trail 234 is about 1 mile north of Rancho Viejo. The trail continues north up the canyon to a ridge and then descends Cañon del Oso to the Rio Frijoles and the junction with Trail 154. After crossing the river, the trail climbs another ridge above the Agua Sarca canyon and drops into the Rito Gallina canyon and the junction with Trail 228. The intersection with Trail 156 is at the top of this ridge. From this point the trail levels off quite a bit and descends gradually to the Rio Medio. The crossing may be tricky during runoff. After the river crossing, the trail makes a short climb out of the canyon to Borrego Mesa.

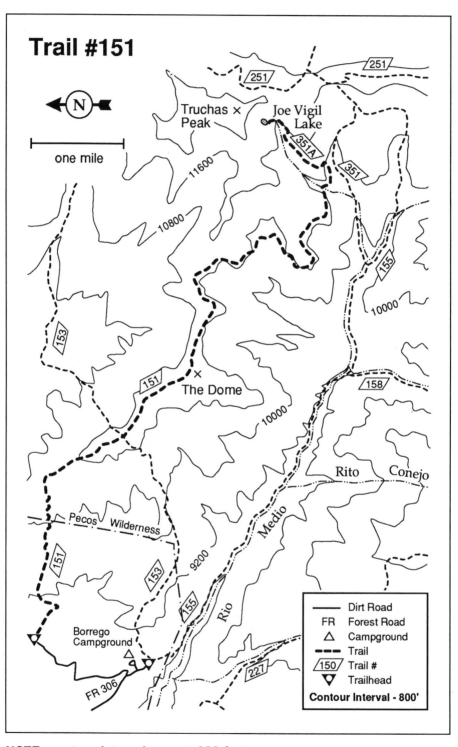

NOTE: contour intervals are at 800 feet

TRAIL 151–DOME TRAIL

LENGTH: 4½ miles to Dome; 5 miles from Dome to Joe Vigil Lake

RATING: Difficult

USE: Light

SEASONS: Late summer to fall

NOTES: Trailhead is very difficult to find; sections of the trail are difficult to find and follow. Travel from Dome to Vigil Lake requires good map and compass skills and involves rugged cross-country travel. ***Not recommended.*** Trailhead is not a safe area to leave a vehicle.

LOCATION: Española Ranger District, Santa Fe National Forest

TRAIL ACCESS: Forest Road 306

USGS MAPS: Sierra Mosca, Truchas Peak

DESCRIPTION: This trail begins off FR 306, near Borrego Mesa. A timber sale in the area has obscured the trailhead and the start of the trail is difficult to find. The trail is a road until it gets near the wilderness boundary (about 1½ miles). Soon after entering the wilderness, the trail heads southeast, traveling through mixed conifer forest. Although the trail is rough and rocky, it is fairly easy to follow with some obscure sections. The trail reaches the Dome, a prominent hill, 4½ miles from the trailhead. The Forest Service map shows the trail continuing from the Dome to Joe Vigil Lake; these last 5 miles of trail are almost impossible to find. Those wishing to continue should have good map and compass skills and be prepared for rugged cross-country travel.

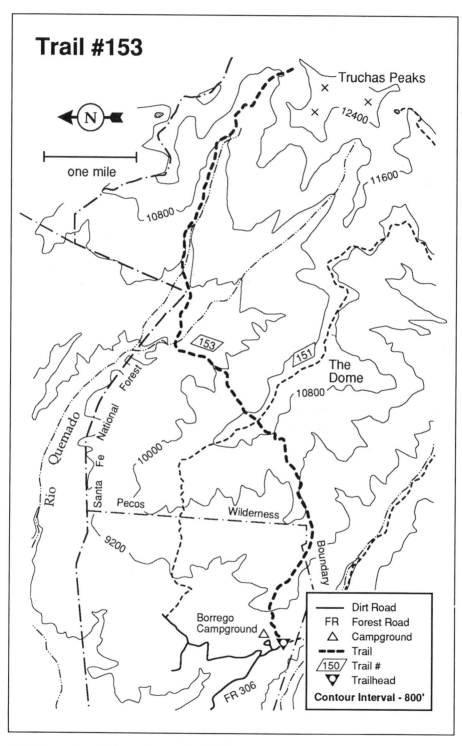

NOTE: contour intervals are at 800 feet

TRAIL 153–QUEMADO TRAIL

LENGTH: 10 miles

RATING: Difficult

USE: Light

SEASONS: Mid-summer to early fall

HIGHEST & LOWEST POINTS: 13,024 ft. & 9,600 ft.

NOTES: This is a lightly used trail, good for those seeking solitude. Parts of it may be difficult to locate due to lack of use, cattle trails, and hikers' spur trails. The climb to North Truchas Peak is extremely strenuous and difficult.

LOCATION: Española Ranger District, Santa Fe National Forest

TRAIL ACCESS: Borrego Mesa Trailhead

USGS MAP: Truchas Peak

DESCRIPTION: From Borrego Mesa Campground, continue to follow the road uphill to the east and northeast for another mile. The road will narrow into a trail after a cabin is reached. The trail climbs along a ridge for 4 miles and reaches the intersection with Trail 151. To continue along Trail 153, the traveler must turn to the northwest down Trail 151 and look for the post marking the continuation of Trail 153. At this point the trail branches off to the northeast and soon begins a rapid descent to the Quemado canyons. The trail crosses several streams and meets an old jeep trail. Continue uphill along this trail for about a mile; it will narrow into a hiking trail. From here the trail will climb steadily along the north fork of the Rio Quemado to the boggy flats just west of the Truchas Peaks ridge, passing a waterfall along the way. There are many spur trails along the tributaries of the Rio Quemado. To stay on Trail 153, follow the trail along the southernmost tributary to its headwaters just below the ridge between North and Middle Truchas peaks. You may wish to continue along a spur trail to the top of North Truchas Peak. This route is not maintained and can be extremely difficult.

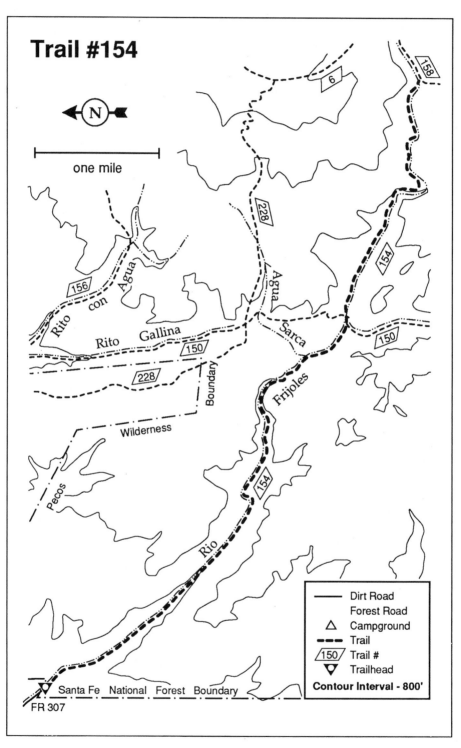

Trail #154

N

one mile

6

158

228

154

156

Rito con Agua

Agua

Sarca

Rito Gallina

150

150

228

Boundary

Frijoles

Wilderness

154

Pecos

Rio

Santa Fe National Forest Boundary

FR 307

	Dirt Road
	Forest Road
△	Campground
---	Trail
150	Trail #
▽	Trailhead
Contour Interval - 800'	

NOTE: contour intervals are at 800 feet

TRAIL 154–FRIJOLES TRAIL

LENGTH: 9 miles

RATING: Moderate

USE: Light

SEASONS: Summer to mid-fall

HIGHEST & LOWEST POINTS: 9,600 ft. & 7,000 ft.

NOTES: The trail is not recommended in late spring and early summer when snow runoff is high. The depth of the river and the strength of the current can make it dangerous to cross. The first mile of trail is a dirt road up the Frijoles drainage. The trail may be difficult to find and follow in the canyon bottom.

LOCATION: Española Ranger District, Santa Fe National Forest

TRAIL ACCESS: Forest Road 307 & Trail 158

USGS MAP: Sierra Mosca

DESCRIPTION: Continue up the closed section of Forest Road 307 on foot, traveling above the river for ½ mile or so. The jeep road eventually fades into a trail. From here on, Trail 154 continues along the Rio Frijoles all the way to its terminus at the intersection of Trail 158. The trail crosses from one side of the river to the other quite frequently and you will get your feet wet! You will encounter the junction with Trail 150 near Cañada Vaca after 6 miles of hiking. Trail 154 continues east in the Frijoles canyon, which begins to widen out after this point. Another 3 miles of canyon hiking will bring you to the trail's end at the junction with Trail 158.

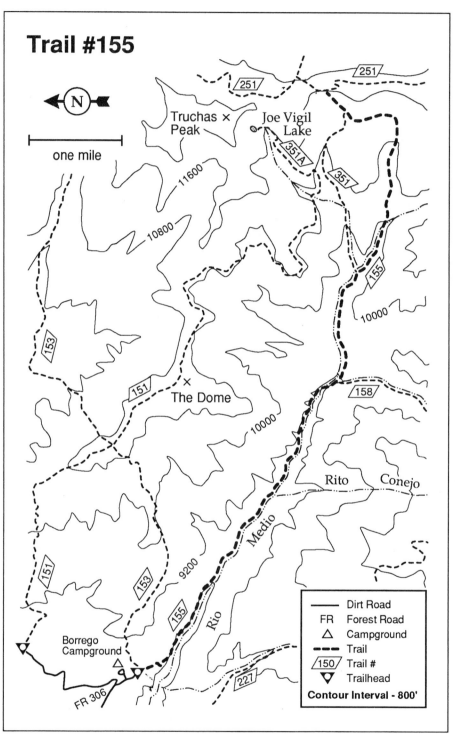

Trail #155

N

one mile

Truchas × Peak

Joe Vigil Lake

251

251

351A

351

11600

10800

155

10000

153

151

The Dome ×

158

10000

Rito   Conejo

Medio

153

9200

151

155

Rio

Borrego Campground

227

	Dirt Road
FR	Forest Road
△	Campground
---	Trail
150	Trail #
▽	Trailhead

Contour Interval - 800'

FR 306

NOTE: contour intervals are at 800 feet

TRAIL 155–RIO MEDIO TRAIL

LENGTH: 10 miles

RATING: Moderate

USE: Moderate

SEASONS: Summer to mid-fall

HIGHEST & LOWEST POINTS: 11,600 ft. & 8,600 ft.

NOTES: This trail offers a less heavily used route to the heart of the Pecos high country with great opportunities for solitude. There are many stream crossings along the way which will slow travel. Prepare to get your feet wet! *All lake basins in the wilderness are closed to camping and campfires.* Overuse has caused severe resource damage in these areas.

LOCATION: Española Ranger District, Santa Fe National Forest

TRAIL ACCESS: Borrego Mesa Trailhead & Trail 251

USGS MAPS: Sierra Mosca, Truchas Peak

DESCRIPTION: From the trailhead at Borrego Mesa, Trail 155 switchbacks quickly down to the canyon bottom and begins to follow the Rio Medio upstream. For the first 5 miles, the trail stays mainly on the north side of the river. At mile 5 the turnoff to Trail 158 is found. Another 2 miles brings the traveler to the junction with Trail 351. Trail 155 continues up the south tributary of the Rio Medio. At the head of the canyon, the trail seems to end in a large boggy field. The trail can be picked up by crossing to the far north end of the field and proceeding upslope to the east. The trail swings north at the top of a ridge near two small lakes and intersects with Trail 351. If the trail has not been picked up before this, it can be found on the outskirts of these lakes to the northeast. From here the trail angles up the west side of Trailriders Wall and joins Skyline Trail (251) on top.

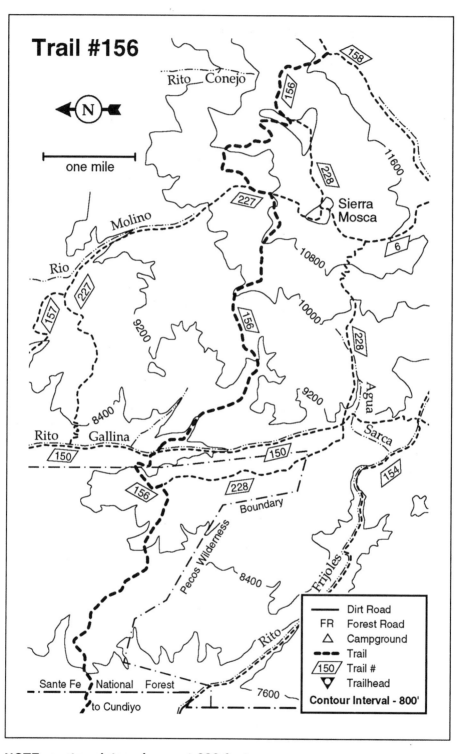

NOTE: contour intervals are at 800 feet

TRAIL 156–RITO CON AGUA TRAIL

LENGTH: 13 miles to private land; 2 miles on private land

RATING: Difficult

USE: Light

SEASONS: Summer to fall

NOTES: Western end of trail is on private land; access may be difficult. Trail is hard to find and follow; heavy treefall makes travel difficult. ***Not recommended, especially for livestock.***

LOCATION: Española Ranger District, Santa Fe National Forest

TRAIL ACCESS: Trail 158 & Cundiyo Trailhead

USGS MAPS: Sierra Mosca, Cundiyo

DESCRIPTION: 156 begins from Trail 158 at the north end of Panchuela Meadows and goes up the Rito Jaroso drainage. This steep climb may be difficult to find in places. Shortly after climbing out of the drainage, the trail meets with Trail 228, then travels through forest for about 1½ miles before meeting Trail 227. The trail is rocky and may be hard to find in this section. 227 and 156 merge for about ½ mile, then 156 turns west while 227 continues south; this junction may be difficult to find. Continue along a ridge before descending into the Rito con Agua drainage and soon intersecting Trail 150. This section has heavy downfall and the trail may be obscured. Shortly after crossing 150, Trail 156 leaves the wilderness and follows a road across national forest land until it reaches private land near the town of Cundiyo. At this point it becomes a trail again and continues about 2½ miles to its western terminus near Cundiyo.

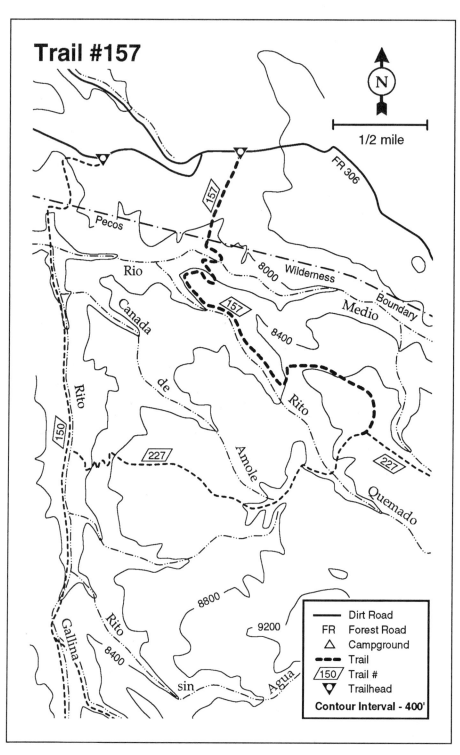

Trail #157

N

1/2 mile

FR 306

157

Pecos

Wilderness

8000

Rio

Boundary

Canada

Medio

157

8400

de

Rito

Rito

150

Amole

227

227

Quemado

8800

9200

Gallina

Rito

8400

sin

Agua

	Dirt Road
FR	Forest Road
△	Campground
▬ ▬	Trail
150	Trail #
▽	Trailhead
Contour Interval - 400'	

NOTE: contour intervals are at 400 feet

TRAIL 157

LENGTH: 3½ miles

RATING: Difficult

USE: Light

SEASONS: Summer to fall

NOTES: It is not safe to leave a vehicle at Borrego Mesa due to vandalism; the Rio Medio crossing is not safe for livestock and *trail is not recommended for livestock* due to heavy downfall. Sections of the trail are difficult to find and follow; trail is not shown on USGS maps.

LOCATION: Española Ranger District, Santa Fe National Forest

TRAIL ACCESS: Forest Road 306 & Trail 227

USGS MAP: Sierra Mosca

DESCRIPTION: This trail begins as a fire road just past a fence marking private land off FR 306. After a mile the trail enters the wilderness and drops down to the Rio Medio. This crossing is hazardous to livestock due to the steepness of the trail on either side of the crossing. The climb out of the Rio Medio is steep and eroded, but the trail then continues on a more moderate grade until it reaches the ridgeline. From the ridgeline to the junction with 227, the trail is obscured by heavy brush. The tread is very difficult to find and follow and is hidden further by considerable downfall.

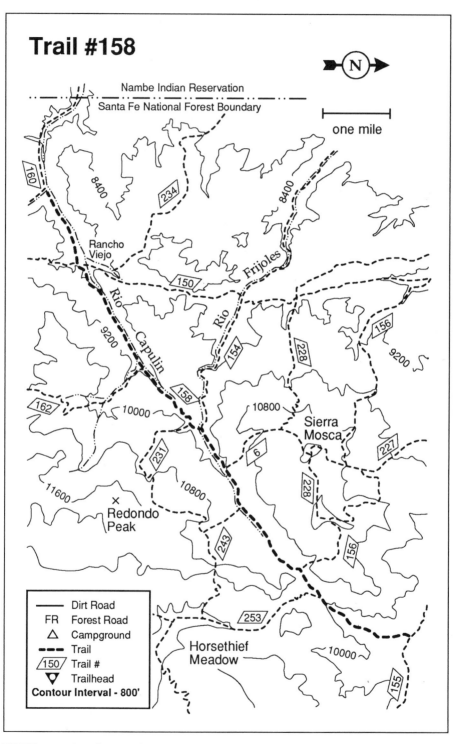

NOTE: contour intervals are at 800 feet

TRAIL 158–CAPULIN TRAIL

LENGTH: 10 miles

RATING: Moderate

USE: Light

SEASONS: Late spring to mid-fall

HIGHEST & LOWEST POINTS: 10,600 ft. & 7,700 ft.

NOTES: This trail has a moderate grade and four major river crossings. Crossings may be difficult during spring runoff due to high water and strong currents. Junctions may be difficult to find.

LOCATION: Española Ranger District, Santa Fe National Forest

TRAIL ACCESS: Trails 160 & 155

USGS MAPS: Sierra Mosca, Aspen Basin, Truchas Peak

DESCRIPTION: Starting from Trail 160 at the junction of the Rio Capulin and Rio Nambe, the trail follows the Rio Capulin for 2 miles and reaches the junction with Trail 150. Trail 158 continues northeast, following the Capulin for 2 miles to the junction with Trail 162. From here Trail 158 turns up a side canyon and continues up the ridge above the Rio Frijoles. At the top of this ridge is the junction with Trail 231. From here Trail 158 drops to the Rio Frijoles and crosses it to meet with Trail 154. Continue northeast on Trail 158 up the Frijoles. You will pass through the open, grassy range called Panchuela West to the old junction with Trail 243 (which no longer exists). Trail 158 begins to climb out of the canyon for 2 miles, reaching its highest point near the intersection with Trail 156. 158 continues northeast, dropping into a small drainage and following it for 3 miles to its terminus at Trail 155.

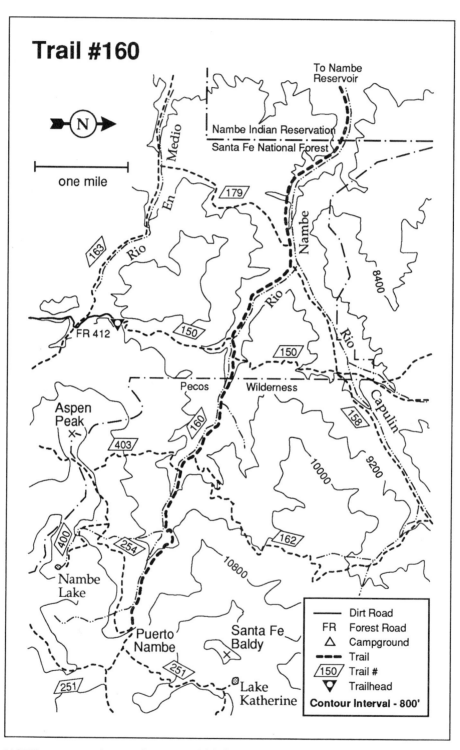

Trail #160

one mile

NOTE: contour intervals are at 800 feet

TRAIL 160–NAMBE TRAIL

LENGTH: 12 miles

RATING: Moderate

USE: Moderate

SEASONS: Late spring to mid-fall

HIGHEST & LOWEST POINTS: 11,000 ft. & 7,100 ft.

NOTES: There are numerous stream crossings, especially in the first 4 miles. The river is quite large at the lower elevations and may be impassable early in the season when runoff is high. ***Not recommended for horses.*** Trail junctions may be obscure.

LOCATION: Española Ranger District, Santa Fe National Forest

TRAIL ACCESS: Nambe Reservoir & Trail 254

USGS MAPS: Tesuque, Aspen Basin

DESCRIPTION: From Nambe Reservoir, pick up the trail at the north end of the dam and follow the river upstream. The first canyon is narrow, with the trail traversing rocky passages along the cliffs above. Then the canyon widens and the trail drops back down to the river level and makes several crossings. The trail continues up the Rio Nambe to the Rio Capulin and Trail 158. Continuing up the Nambe for 2 miles will bring you to Trail 150, then go east up the Nambe for another 2 miles to the junctions with Trails 162 and 403. The trail travels through large meadows in its last 1½ miles and climbs up to join Trail 254 just below the flat, grassy mesa of Puerto Nambe.

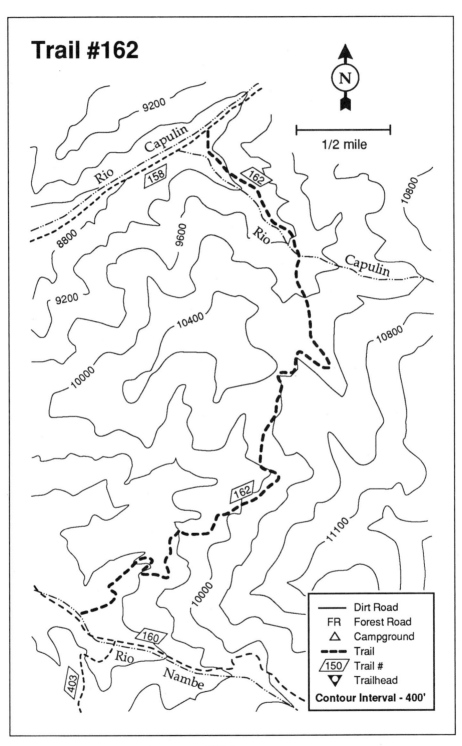

Trail #162

N

1/2 mile

9200

Rio Capulin

158

162

Rio

Capulin

10800

10800

9200

9600

10400

10000

162

11100

10000

160

Rio

Nambe

403

Dirt Road

FR **Forest Road**

△ **Campground**

- - - **Trail**

150 **Trail #**

▽ **Trailhead**

Contour Interval - 400'

NOTE: contour intervals are at 400 feet

TRAIL 162–CAPULIN CIENEGA TRAIL

LENGTH: 7 miles

RATING: Difficult

USE: Light

SEASONS: Late spring to mid-fall

HIGHEST & LOWEST POINTS: 10,400 ft. & 8,800 ft.

NOTES: This is an infrequently maintained trail and is difficult to find and follow in places. The climb out of the Rio Nambe canyon is very steep and difficult. Junctions may be obscure. Recommended for experienced hikers only.

LOCATION: Española Ranger District, Santa Fe National Forest

TRAIL ACCESS: Trails 160 & 158

USGS MAP: Aspen Basin

DESCRIPTION: From Trail 160, this trail takes a steep climb out of the Rio Nambe drainage, following a side canyon then turning west and climbing steeply up the hillside. The trail goes through a mixed conifer forest for 2 miles to a ridgetop. After a short downhill, the trail resumes its uphill trend and, after several stream crossings, enters an aspen grove. The trail may be difficult to find and follow at this point. Trail 162 goes north through the aspen grove and is less obvious than hunting trails. The trail switchbacks uphill, crossing a small meadow. The trail then gets easier to follow, continuing to a ridgetop, dropping down along the northern side, then turning and heading toward the Rio Capulin. The trail arrives at a large marsh and is picked up by circling the marsh on the north side and proceeding to the easternmost side. You will soon reach a small meadow. The trail continues at the far northeast corner of the meadow and is easily followed downhill to the intersection with Trail 158. There are numerous stream crossings along the way.

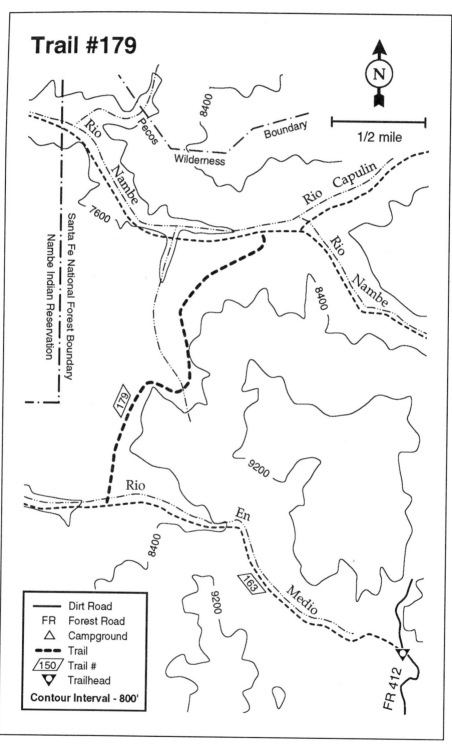

Trail #179

N

1/2 mile

Rio Pecos

Wilderness
Boundary

Rio Nambe

Rio Capulin

Rio Nambe

7600

8400

8400

Santa Fe National Forest Boundary

Nambe Indian Reservation

179

9200

Rio

En

Medio

163

9200

8400

FR 412

———	Dirt Road
FR	Forest Road
△	Campground
- - -	Trail
150	Trail #
▽	Trailhead

Contour Interval - 800'

NOTE: contour intervals are at 800 feet

TRAIL 179

LENGTH: 2½ miles

RATING: Moderate

USE: Light

SEASONS: Summer to fall

NOTES: This trail is not in the wilderness.

LOCATION: Española Ranger District, Santa Fe National Forest

TRAIL ACCESS: Trails 160 & 163

USGS MAP: Aspen Basin

DESCRIPTION: This trail connects the Rio en Medio and Rio Nambe and is easy to find and follow. From Trail 160, Trail 179 travels southwest through ponderosa pine forest. After about 1 mile the trail crosses a small drainage and then passes beneath a powerline. Another mile brings you to the Rio en Medio. A section of trail just north of the Rio en Medio has been washed away and the trail now follows an arroyo. Shortly after crossing the Rio en Medio the trail ends at the junction with Trail 163.

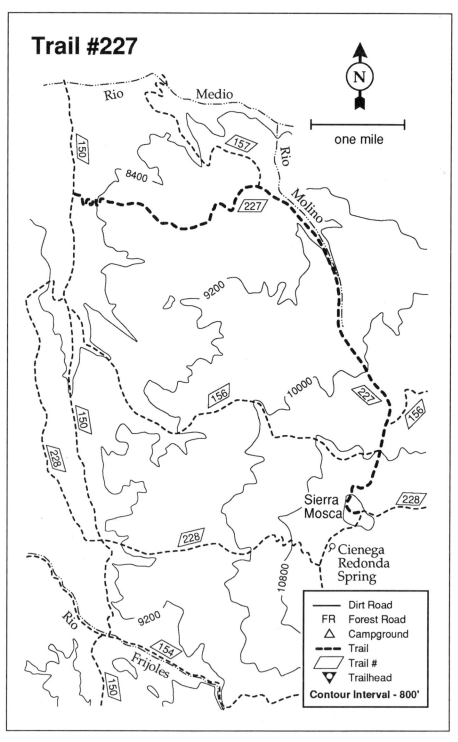

TRAIL 227–AMOLE TRAIL

LENGTH: 6 miles

RATING: Difficult

USE: Light

SEASONS: Summer to fall

NOTES: **This trail is not recommended;** it is extremely difficult to find and follow; good navigation skills are a must. Cross-country travel may be needed to complete the hike.

LOCATION: Española Ranger District, Santa Fe National Forest

TRAIL ACCESS: Trails 150 & 228

USGS MAPS: Sierra Mosca

DESCRIPTION: Trail 227 heads east from an obscure junction with Trail 150. The trail climbs out of the Rito Gallina canyon by a series of steep switchbacks, reaches the Rio Molino after 2½ miles, and continues up the river for about 2 miles. This section of trail is fairly easy to follow but there are many downed trees. The trail leaves the Rio Molino, climbing through mixed conifer forest on a path that is very brushy, rocky, and hard to follow. The trail continues past the two obscure junctions with Trail 156 to its terminus at Trail 228 near Sierra Mosca.

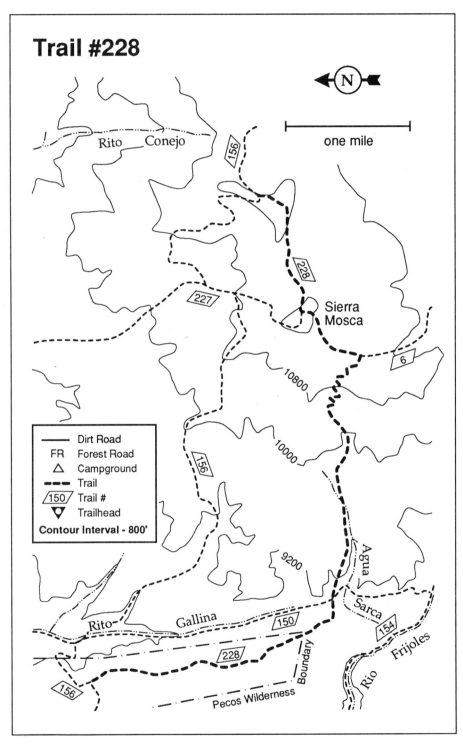

Trail #228

Rito Conejo

one mile

156

228

Sierra Mosca

227

6

10800

156

10000

9200

Agua Sarca

Rito Gallina

150

228

154

Rio Frijoles

156

Boundary

Pecos Wilderness

Dirt Road
FR Forest Road
△ Campground
- - - Trail
150 Trail #
▽ Trailhead
Contour Interval - 800'

NOTE: contour intervals are at 800 feet

TRAIL 228

LENGTH: 13 miles

RATING: Difficult

USE: Light

SEASONS: Late spring to mid-fall

HIGHEST & LOWEST POINTS: 11,600 ft. & 8,600 ft.

NOTES: The first 3 miles of Trail 228 is an old jeep road closed to motor vehicles. The trail is infrequently maintained and may have heavy tree-fall, making travel difficult, especially for horses. Much of the trail has disappeared over the years and navigation through this area can be challenging. *The visitor must have good orienteering skills to negotiate this trail. This trail is not recommended.*

LOCATION: Española Ranger District, Santa Fe National Forest

TRAIL ACCESS: Trail 156, west and east junctions

USGS MAP: Sierra Mosca

DESCRIPTION: From the western junction with Trail 156, Trail 228 climbs rapidly out of the canyon and intersects with an old jeep road. Follow this road and after 3 miles it intersects with Trail 150. The road narrows to a trail and continues east above the Agua Sarca River. The trail becomes difficult to find and follow in this section. It generally continues up the drainage. The trail follows a ridge north of the drainage and soon swings toward the headwaters of the Agua Sarca. From here the trail switchbacks up the slope to a flat, grassy mesa and may easily be lost. Follow a ridge to the north and drop into Cienega Redonda and the junction with Trail 6. Trail 228 continues northeast and skirts the side of Sierra Mosca, turns north and drops to a grassy saddle. The sign at this saddle is incorrect; the turnoff to Panchuela West is several miles to the east. From here the trail crosses meadows and finally emerges on a flat, grassy mesa near the eastern junction with Trail 156.

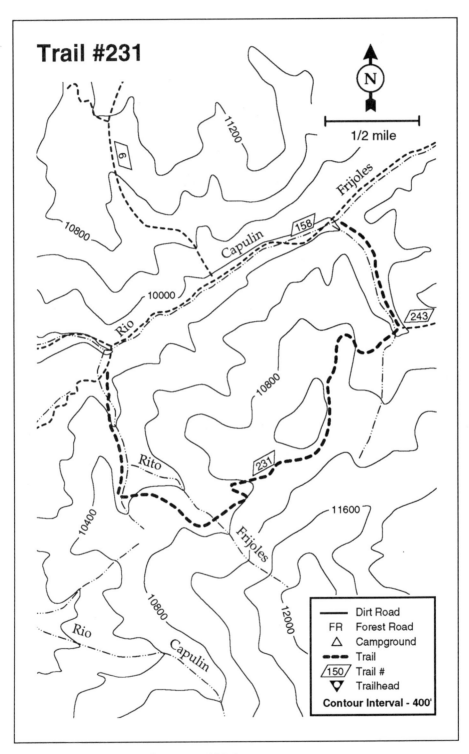

NOTE: contour intervals are at 400 feet

TRAIL 231

LENGTH: 3½ miles

RATING: Difficult

USE: Light

SEASONS: Summer to fall

NOTES: **Not recommended.** Much of this trail is obscure; heavy downfall makes travel difficult for hikers and impossible for horses. The trail is not shown on USGS maps.

LOCATION: Española Ranger District, Santa Fe National Forest

TRAIL ACCESS: Trail 158

USGS MAPS: Sierra Mosca, Aspen Basin

DESCRIPTION: The trail begins near Panchuela West at the eastern junction with Trail 158. Trail 231 crosses the Rio Frijoles and travels up a small drainage; this is a moderate climb up a steep, narrow canyon. After about a mile, the trail turns southwest and leaves the drainage. The junction with old Trail 243 was near this turn (243 has been abandoned and closed). From this point 231 becomes difficult to find and follow. The trail travels through forests with small openings and has steep, rugged sections. It eventually drops down to the Rito Frijoles, following the drainage for about 1 mile before rejoining Trail 158 at the western junction.

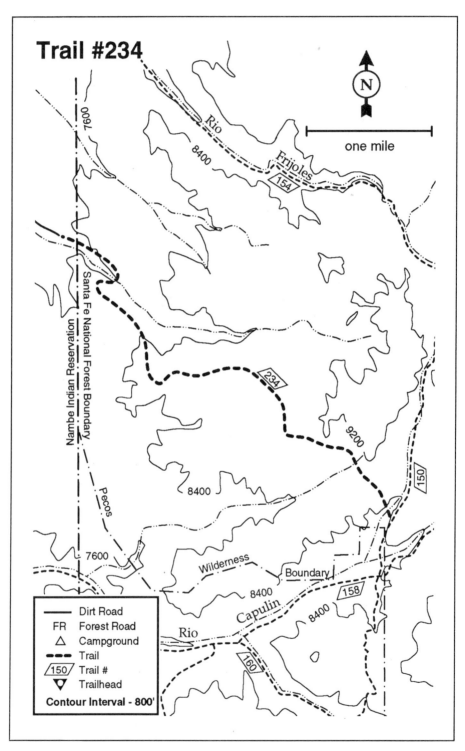

NOTE: contour intervals are at 800 feet

TRAIL 234

LENGTH: 5 miles

RATING: Moderate

USE: Light

SEASONS: Late spring to late fall

NOTES: Both ends of the trail are very steep and may be hard to find. There is no public parking at the Boy Scout camp on the western end; you must call the Boy Scout office in Albuquerque to get permission. There is little water along the trail—carry plenty. The trail is not shown on USGS maps.

LOCATION: Española Ranger District, Santa Fe National Forest

TRAIL ACCESS: Trail 150 & Frank Rand Boy Scout Camp

USGS MAPS: Aspen Basin, Sierra Mosca

DESCRIPTION: From Trail 150, Trail 234 crosses the Cañada Vaca and heads uphill to the northwest. This first portion is very steep and may be difficult to find. When it reaches the ridgetop, the trail continues on gently rolling terrain but may be hard to find and follow in places along the ridge due to lack of use. The next 3½ miles pass through mixed conifer forest at higher elevations and piñon-juniper toward the west end. This trail offers outstanding views of Santa Fe Baldy, Redondo, Lake, and Penitente peaks to the east and the Jemez Mountains to the west. 234 drops off the ridge in the last mile, crossing a small canyon and making a very steep descent to its terminus at the Boy Scout camp.

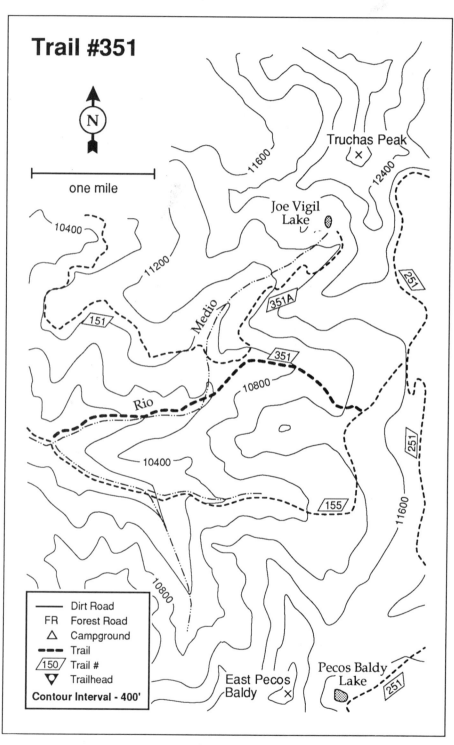

Trail #351

N

one mile

Truchas Peak ×

11600

12400

Joe Vigil Lake

10400

11200

251

Medio

351A

151

Rio

351

10800

10400

251

155

11600

10800

Dirt Road
FR Forest Road
△ Campground
- - - Trail
150 Trail #
▽ Trailhead
Contour Interval - 400'

Pecos Baldy Lake

East Pecos Baldy ×

251

NOTE: contour intervals are at 400 feet

TRAIL 351

LENGTH: 3 miles

RATING: Difficult

USE: Light

SEASONS: Summer to mid-fall

HIGHEST & LOWEST POINTS: 11,600 ft. & 9,600 ft.

*NOTES: **All lake basins in the wilderness are closed to camping and campfires.*** Overuse has caused severe resource damage in these areas.

LOCATION: Española Ranger District, Santa Fe National Forest

TRAIL ACCESS: 155, west & east ends

USGS MAP: Truchas Peak

DESCRIPTION: From Trail 155, continue east up the Rio Medio. After 1½ miles a grassy plateau is encountered. Trail 151/351A goes north at this point. Trail 351 continues east up the canyon to a couple of small boggy lakes at the base of Trailriders Wall. The trail joins with Trail 155 near these lakes and terminates at Trailriders Wall. Trail 151/351A takes a side trip to Joe Vigil Lake. This route is difficult to follow, as several routes exist and the tread becomes faint or nonexistent. Travel to the lake is cross-country.

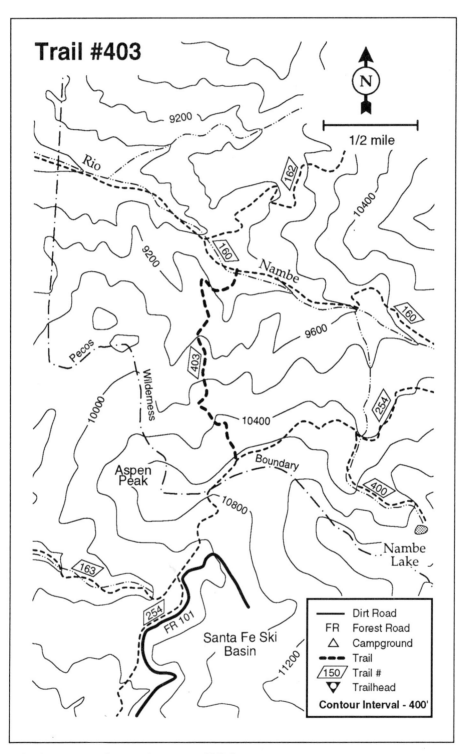

NOTE: contour intervals are at 400 feet

TRAIL 403

LENGTH: 1½ miles

RATING: Difficult

USE: Light

SEASONS: Midsummer through fall

NOTES: The junctions are very difficult to find. The trail is extremely steep; heavy downfall may slow travel. ***This trail is not recommended.***

LOCATION: Española Ranger District, Santa Fe National Forest

TRAIL ACCESS: Trails 254 & 160

USGS MAP: Aspen Basin

DESCRIPTION: The junction with Trail 254 is very, very difficult to find. The tread and blazes are obscure and the junction sign is 10 feet up in a tree. Look carefully; this junction is obscure on the ground. The trail descends through heavy spruce forest into the Rio Nambe drainage and is extremely steep and rocky.

NORTHERN SECTION
TRAILHEADS

Trailheads are not patrolled. Do not leave valuable items in your vehicle. Do not leave your vehicle parked unattended for extended periods of time. You may wish to arrange shuttles or drop-offs. If your vehicle is broken into or vandalized, notify the Forest Service and the county sheriff.

SANTA BARBARA: Take State Highway 76 through the towns of Chimayo and Truchas to Highway 75 and then to Highway 73 *or* take State Highway 75 north of Española and travel through Dixon to Peñasco. From Peñasco continue along State Highway 73/Forest Road 116 to Santa Barbara Campground. The last few miles from Peñasco are over a well-maintained dirt road. Camping, corrals, and water are available for a fee. The trail begins across the road from the wilderness parking area. *Access to Trail 24 and from there to Trail 25.*

LAS TRAMPAS: Take State Highway 76 northeast of Española. Just north of the town of Las Trampas look for the turnoff to Forest Road 207. This is a well-maintained dirt road traveling approximately 8 miles to Trampas Campground. About ½ mile before the end of the road take Forest Road 639 one mile to Trail 30. To get to Trail 31, continue on FR 207. Camping and picnicking are available at the campground. There is no fee. *Access to Trails 30 and 31.*

RIPLEY POINT: From Peñasco take State Highway 518 toward Tres Ritos. Park at Agua Piedra Campground just before Tres Ritos. Follow the logging road on Trails 19, 22, and 36 to Ripley Point. *Access to Trails 19, 22, and 36.*

ALAMITOS: Take State Highway 518 about 6 miles south of Tres Ritos to Forest Road 161. Turn southwest on this road and follow it to its end. Limited parking is available. *Access to Trails 19 and from there to 36.*

The maps accompanying the trail descriptions are for orientation only. For a more detailed representation of topographic features, please refer to the wilderness map or appropriate USGS quadrangles.

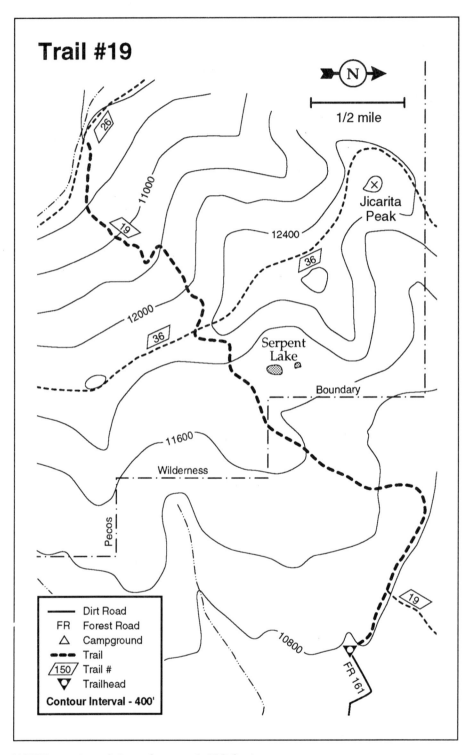

NOTE: contour intervals are at 400 feet

TRAIL 19–AGUA PIEDRA TRAIL

LENGTH: 11½ miles

RATING: Moderate

USE: Moderate

SEASONS: Late summer to fall

*NOTES: **All lake basins are closed to camping and campfires due to resource damage.***

LOCATION: Camino Real Ranger District, Carson National Forest

TRAIL ACCESS: Trail 26 & Forest Road 708

USGS MAPS: Jicarita Peak, Holman

DESCRIPTION: From the junction with Trail 26 at the East Fork Rio Santa Barbara, Trail 19 makes a steep and difficult climb up the Jicarita Peak ridge and then drops down the east side of the ridge. A spur trail takes a side trip to Serpent Lake. From this point Trail 19 heads downhill to the northeast and widens into a road soon after leaving the wilderness. Much of the rest of the distance to Agua Piedra Campground is a primitive road rather than a trail. Multiple roads and intersections can make navigation difficult. ***The northern half of Trail 19 to Agua Piedra Campground and FR 708 is not shown on this map.***

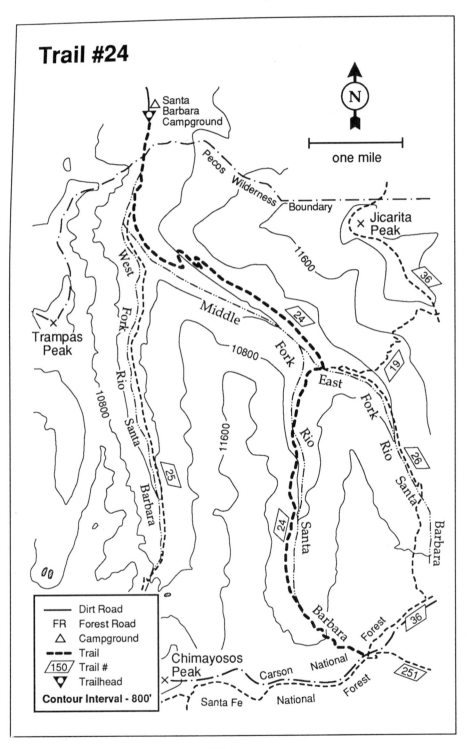

NOTE: contour intervals are at 800 feet

TRAIL 24–MIDDLE FORK TRAIL

LENGTH: 12 miles

RATING: Moderate

USE: Light

SEASONS: Mid-summer to mid-fall

HIGHEST & LOWEST POINTS: 12,000 ft. & 8,900 ft.

NOTES: The terrain is wet and bogs will be encountered frequently along the way.

LOCATION: Camino Real Ranger District, Carson National Forest

TRAIL ACCESS: Santa Barbara Campground & Trail 251

USGS MAPS: Jicarita Peak, Pecos Falls

DESCRIPTION: From the campground, take Trail 24 south and follow it southeast up the Middle Fork of the Rio Santa Barbara. This trail climbs up the hillside to the north of the drainage above the river. After 3 miles the trail drops back down into the drainage. The junction with Trails 19 and 26 is found near the intersection of the East and Middle Forks of the Rio Santa Barbara. Trail 24 heads up the canyon on the east side of the middle fork drainage. The trail continues up the canyon, crossing to the west side of the drainage. Many maps show the trail remaining on the east side of the creek, but the trail actually remains on the west side for the last 3 to 4 miles as it climbs to the divide. The trail also crosses occasional tributaries flowing down the hillside. These stream crossings and bogs may slow travel. Trail 24 continues up the canyon to the Santa Barbara Divide and down the other side.

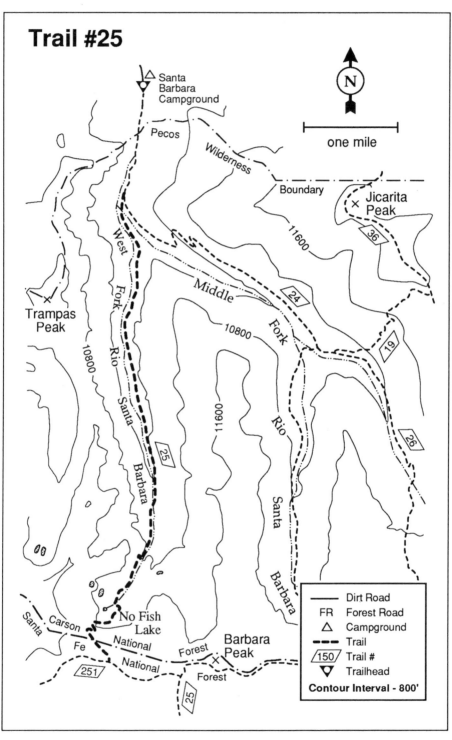

Trail #25

Santa Barbara Campground

Pecos

Wilderness

Boundary

Jicarita Peak

36

11600

West Fork

Middle Fork

24

Trampas Peak

Rio

10800

Santa

10800

Fork

19

Barbara

11600

Rio

Santa

25

26

Barbara

No Fish Lake

Santa

Carson

Fe National

National Forest

Barbara Peak

Forest

Forest

251

25

	Dirt Road
FR	Forest Road
△	Campground
- - -	Trail
150	Trail #
▽	Trailhead

Contour Interval - 800'

NOTE: contour intervals are at 800 feet

TRAIL 25-WEST FORK TRAIL

LENGTH: 8 miles

RATING: Moderate

USE: Moderate

SEASONS: Mid-summer to early fall

HIGHEST & LOWEST POINTS: 11,600 ft. & 9,300 ft.

NOTES: This is the most heavily used trail from Santa Barbara Campground. *All lake basins in the wilderness are closed to camping and campfires.* This is to protect the fragile environment.

LOCATION: Camino Real Ranger District, Carson National Forest

TRAIL ACCESS: Trail 24 & Trail 25, Part 2

USGS MAPS: Jicarita Peak, Pecos Falls

DESCRIPTION: From Trail 24, this trail branches south and goes up the West Fork of the Rio Santa Barbara. About ¼ mile south of the junction, 25 crosses the middle fork on a logjam. Use caution when crossing. The west fork canyon begins to narrow as you travel south. After 4 miles cross to the west side of the creek. From here the trail ascends high above the river by way of a series of long, gentle switchbacks. Chimayosos Peak dominates the view to the northeast as the trail continues to climb up the canyon. The final ascent to the Santa Barbara Divide is accomplished by another series of long switchbacks climbing up the barren, rocky slope. The trail terminates at the top of the divide in the saddle between Chimayosos Peak and North Truchas Peak. You can continue on Trail 251 east for 1½ miles to the southern part of Trail 25.

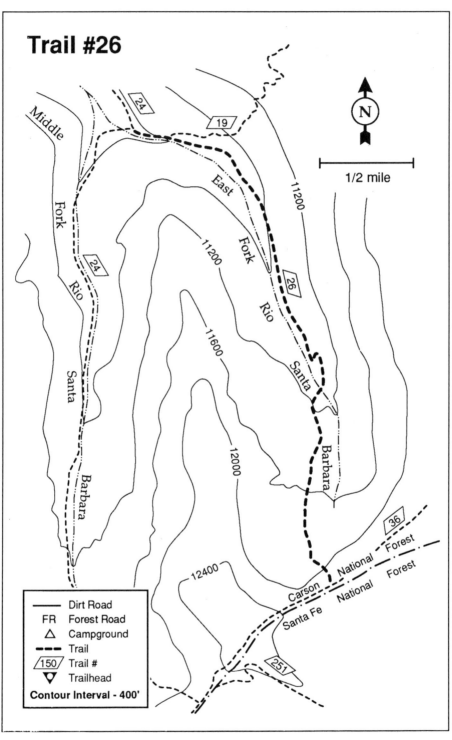

Trail #26

Middle

Fork

Rio

Santa

Barbara

East

Fork

Rio

Santa

Barbara

24

19

11200

26

11200

11600

12000

12400

36

Carson National Forest

Santa Fe National Forest

251

N

1/2 mile

Dirt Road
FR   Forest Road
△   Campground
‐ ‐ ‐   Trail
150   Trail #
▽   Trailhead

Contour Interval – 400'

NOTE: contour intervals are at 400 feet

TRAIL 26–EAST FORK TRAIL

LENGTH: 4½ miles

RATING: Difficult

USE: Light

SEASONS: Mid-summer to early fall

HIGHEST & LOWEST POINTS: 12,100 ft. & 10,300 ft.

NOTES: This trail offers good opportunities for solitude. The trail may disappear in the meadows near the divide and visitors must rely on cairns and stakes to navigate the remaining distance to the top of the divide. Inclement weather or dense fog may make travel difficult or impossible.

LOCATION: Camino Real Ranger District, Carson National Forest

TRAIL ACCESS: Trails 24 & 36

USGS MAPS: Jicarita Peak, Pecos Falls

DESCRIPTION: From the junction with Trail 24, Trail 26 heads up the East Fork Rio Santa Barbara. The trail gradually swings south up another canyon between two ridges coming off the Santa Barbara Divide. The trail travels through open meadows alternating with mixed conifer forests and aspen groves. Higher up the canyon the trail begins to cross various tributaries flowing into the east fork. Near the base of the divide, the terrain flattens out into a series of marshy plateaus. The trail will be hard to find in this area. The final climb to the top of the divide brings the visitor to a saddle east of Barbara Peak and overlooking Rincon Bonito to the south. This section of the trail to the divide has no marks and is very hard to find. You may need a compass. The trail terminates on the divide at Trail 36.

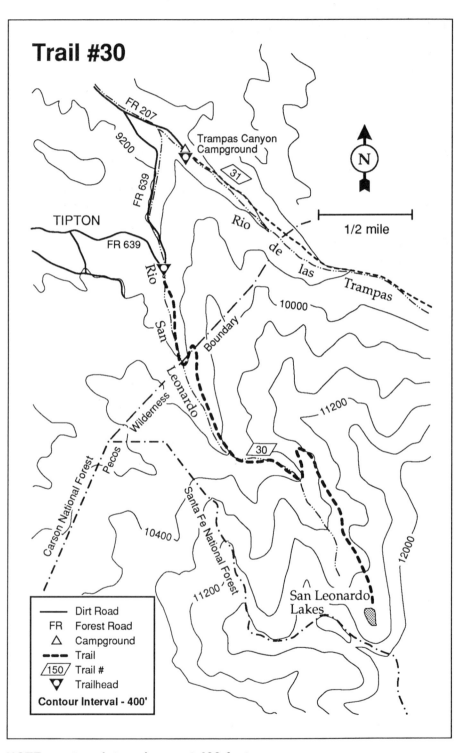

NOTE: contour intervals are at 400 feet

TRAIL 30

LENGTH: 6 miles

RATING: Moderate

USE: Light

SEASONS: Summer to mid-fall

HIGHEST & LOWEST POINTS: 11,280 ft. & 9,280 ft.

*NOTES: **All lake basins in the wilderness are closed to camping and camp-fires.*** This is to protect the fragile environment of the basins.

LOCATION: Camino Real Ranger District, Carson National Forest

TRAIL ACCESS: Forest Road 639 (Trampas Trailhead)

USGS MAP: El Valle

DESCRIPTION: From the trailhead, the trail climbs up the Rio San Leonardo canyon, becoming steeper the farther you go. Dense conifer forests characterize the route with occasional views of the high mountain ridges to the south and east. The trail terminates at the lake basin.

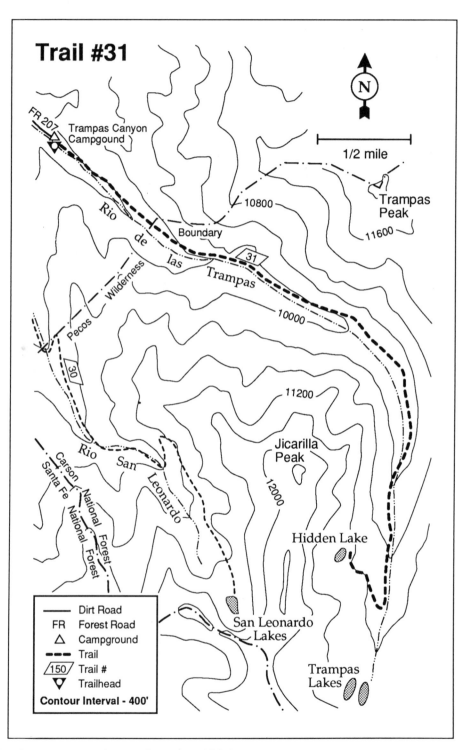

Trail #31

N

1/2 mile

FR 207
Trampas Canyon
Campgound

Rio de las Trampas

10800

Boundary

31

Trampas Peak

11600

Pecos Wilderness

10000

30

11200

Rio San Leonardo

Jicarilla Peak

12000

Carson National Forest
Santa Fe National Forest

Hidden Lake

San Leonardo Lakes

Trampas Lakes

——	Dirt Road
FR	Forest Road
△	Campground
– – –	Trail
150	Trail #
▽	Trailhead
Contour Interval - 400'	

NOTE: contour intervals are at 400 feet

TRAIL 31

LENGTH: 7 miles

RATING: Moderate

USE: Light

SEASONS: Summer to mid-fall

HIGHEST & LOWEST POINTS: 11,200 ft. & 9,200 ft.

NOTES: **All lake basins in the wilderness are closed to camping and campfires.** This is to protect the fragile environment of the basins.

LOCATION: Camino Real Ranger District, Carson National Forest

TRAIL ACCESS: Forest Road 207 at Trampas Canyon Campground

USGS MAPS: El Valle, Truchas Peak

DESCRIPTION: From the campground, the trail begins with a moderate to easy climb up the Trampas canyon. After a couple of miles the canyon opens up into a wide valley. Trail 31 begins a steeper climb after this with a few switchbacks up the more difficult sections. The trail continues up the canyon and terminates near the lake basins.

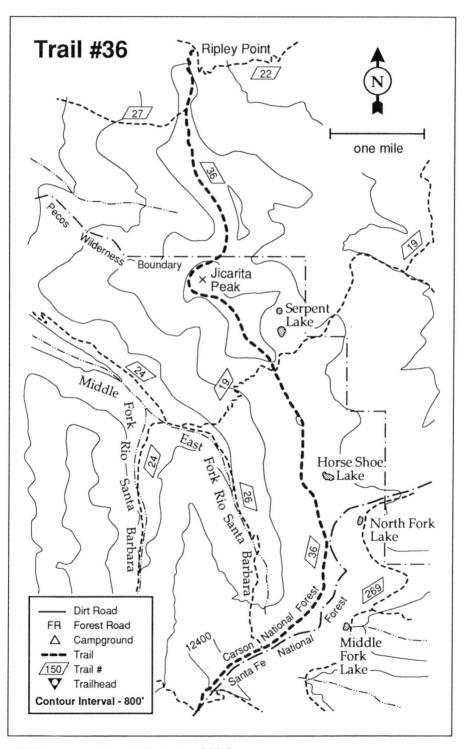

NOTE: contour intervals are at 800 feet

TRAIL 36–NORTH FORK TRAIL

LENGTH: 12 miles

RATING: Difficult

USE: Light

SEASONS: Mid-summer to early fall

HIGHEST & LOWEST POINTS: 12,100 ft. & 11,400 ft.

NOTES: Due to rocky areas and the alpine meadows of this high-altitude ridge, a trail tread may be hard to find and follow. The hiker must be prepared for uneven and rough terrain underfoot.

LOCATION: Camino Real Ranger District, Carson National Forest

TRAIL ACCESS: Trails 22 & 24/251

USGS MAPS: Jicarita Peak, Pecos Falls

DESCRIPTION: Starting from Ripley Point and Trail 22, Trail 36 climbs to a wooded peak on the ridge and then drops to another saddle. The trail continues climbing through conifer forests and occasional meadows along the ridge. After 4 miles, the trail comes out of the trees onto the open ridge which extends all the way to the Santa Barbara Divide. The trail curves around the west side of Jicarita Peak and reaches the junction with Trail 19 two miles later. The trail continues with minor ups and downs along the ridge all the way to the Santa Barbara Divide and its terminus at Trails 24/251.

WILDLIFE

WILDLIFE

One of the most rewarding experiences of a wilderness trip is to observe wildlife. Elk grazing in a meadow, a bear ambling across a slope, a bighorn silhouetted against the sky—these are sights one treasures for a long time.

The keys to successful wildlife viewing are silence, stillness, patience, and knowledge of the animal's habits.

SILENCE: Travel in small groups and avoid making noise. When alone, walk carefully and quietly in the woods, stopping frequently for long periods, looking and listening.

STILLNESS: Find a good vantage point where you will blend into the background, get comfortable, and remain still. Wear clothes that will make you part of the forest; animals are color blind but they do pick up sharp contrasts.

PATIENCE: Wait, wait, and wait some more.

KNOWLEDGE: Dawn and dusk are the best times for observing wildlife. This is when many animals are actively feeding and moving about. The least likely time to encounter wildlife is between 10 a.m. and 4 p.m.; this is a good time to be on the trail. Being in the right habitat is essential. The following pages describe where you are most likely to encounter certain species.

Generally, birds are the most commonly observed wildlife. Mammals are secretive by nature and, aside from squirrels, chipmunks, and marmots, sightings are not common. Binoculars can be a great help for identification; so can the field guides recommended in the suggested reading list of this guidebook. Tracks in muddy areas or snow will tell a great deal about the wildlife that's been around—if you know how to read the signs.

Unless you have a highly trained and obedient dog, leave it home; you are more likely to see wildlife when Fido is not around. Bones, antlers, feathers, and flowers are part of the natural environment; they provide nutrients to the soil when they decompose. Please leave them.

M A M M A L S

MULE DEER (*Odocoileus hemionus*)

Except for the areas above timberline, mule deer are found throughout the Pecos Wilderness. Named for their long ears, mule deer tend to be solitary, though bucks often form small bachelor groups. During the mating season in late fall (October and November) does and fawns are joined by one or two males; after breeding the groups break apart and the bucks go off on their own. Following a gestation period of about seven months, does give birth to one or two fawns, usually in June or July. The young stay with their mothers for one to two years.

Mule deer are browsers; they feed on forbs and shrubs rather than grasses. Since this food is not readily available during winter, deer often lose weight and are under stress. Many young and old individuals die in late winter and early spring. Those that were in the best nutritional condition prior to winter will survive to breed and grow another year.

COYOTE (*Canis latrans*)

The coyote is found throughout the Pecos Wilderness. This small, doglike animal weighs about 25 pounds and is brown to gray in color. It feeds mainly on rodents and other small mammals but also eats fruit and insects.

Mating occurs in late winter or early spring. The female gives birth to a litter of four to six pups in an underground den after a gestation period of approximately two months.

The coyote usually hunts alone but will occasionally hunt in packs. It is most active in the early morning and late afternoon hours. It runs with its tail down, helping to distinguish it from the fox, which carries its tail straight.

The Pecos was once home to the timber wolf (*Canis lupus*) but, like the grizzly bear, the wolf was exterminated. In the wolf's absence, the coyote has expanded its range. Its "singing" evokes memories of the long-gone wolf and, for many people, is the essence of wilderness.

ROCKY MOUNTAIN ELK (*Cervus elaphus*)

The extinct Southwest elk, *Cervus merriami*, was exterminated from New Mexico by 1909. Reintroduction began shortly after with elk from the Yellowstone area, *Cervus elaphus*. Some consider the two types of elk to be two distinct species while others consider Merriam's elk to have been a local race of *C. elaphus*.

Also known as *wapiti*, the elk male is referred to as a bull and the female as a cow. In the Pecos Wilderness, the social unit consists of a herd of cows and calves numbering from 20 to over 100. In May or June, after a gestation period of about eight and a half months, the female leaves the herd to give birth to one or two calves. In a few days, the young join the herd with their mother. The bull is more solitary at this time.

The elk's diet is similar to that of the domestic cow—grasses, sedges, and shrubs. The elk may be encountered grazing in higher elevation mountain meadows during the summer. As autumn approaches, the bull's antlers reach full development and a change in behavior takes place. The bull becomes extremely aggressive, attempting to acquire and defend a harem of from 15 to 30 cows for mating. During this September and October breeding season, the bull uses loud, unique vocalizations called "bugling" to announce its presence to other males and receptive females. By November, the antlers are shed (only the bull develops antlers) and the bull leaves the company of the cows.

When the snow flies, the elk migrate to their winter ranges, where topography and prevailing winds combine to create snow-free meadows for feeding and resting. With the coming of spring, the cycle begins anew.

The best places to see elk herds in summer are along the upper Rio Valdez and upper south fork of the Rio de la Casa along Rincon Bonito; in winter, herds are found from Round Mountain to Jacks Creek Campground.

ROCKY MOUNTAIN BIGHORN SHEEP
(*Ovis canadensis*)

These wild sheep were once common throughout the Sangre de Cristo Mountains. Overhunting and competition and disease from domestic livestock had wiped them out by 1905. The New Mexico Department of Game and Fish reintroduced the bighorn to the Pecos in 1965–66. The herd now numbers about 120.

Herds of ewes and lambs are seen most commonly between Pecos Baldy Lake and Truchas Lakes. The large bachelor-ram herd frequents much rougher country but can be occasionally observed along the Santa Barbara Divide. This reintroduced herd is used to humans. Ewes will enter tents and steal food, so take appropriate precautions. Do not feed these wild sheep; it interferes with proper nutrition and keeps them pesky. Being chased by pet dogs is very stressful to the sheep, as is chasing them on horseback. Keep your dog on a leash when in bighorn habitat.

Wild sheep are highly social. During the fall rut (November and December) the males engage in head-bashing contests to establish dominance. The dominant male breeds with the most females. Gestation takes about 175 days, and most births occur in June. When her time arrives, the female leaves the herd to seek a rugged area safe from predators where she will give birth to one or occasionally two lambs. Lambs begin eating solid food at two weeks of age, consuming mostly grasses and some browse. Minerals are generally obtained from natural salt licks, but these seem to be in short supply in their preferred wilderness range here. They have been known to approach and lick horses for the salty perspiration!

Sheep generally feed in the morning and always stay near a source of drinking water. The bighorn prefers open feeding slopes near rugged, rocky areas where it can escape from predators.

BLACK BEAR (*Ursus americanus*)

The last grizzly bear in New Mexico was shot in 1938, so if you see a bear, it is the black bear. Unfortunately, the black bear comes in many colors—red, brown, cinnamon, and black. There are not many bears at higher elevations in the wilderness. Look for bear sign—tracks, clawed trees, scat, overturned rocks—in mixed conifer or aspen forest, its preferred habitat in the wilderness. Aspen bark is like a book, containing records of visitors, both two- and four-footed.

In spring, the bear feeds on grasses and insects. Summer foods include mammals, insects, and berries. Fall diet is berries and mast (acorns and other nuts). Bears mate in June or July but the embryo does not implant and develop in the mother's uterus until November. This is approximately when denning for the winter occurs. The bear goes into a deep sleep, but is not a true hibernator because its body temperature does not drop drastically. It may wake from this sleep and make short trips outside.

Cubs are born in the den about the end of January and are only six to eight inches long! They first leave the den in March or April and remain with their mother through the next winter. They disperse the following spring.

The adult bear is solitary. It is most active in the evening, often covering several miles a night while foraging. It will rest during the day, seeking shelter among boulders or logs. A black bear can weigh up to 500 pounds and reach about five feet in length.

Never feed or approach a bear. If you see cubs, the mother is near and will be very protective. Look around carefully for the female and back away quietly. To minimize conflicts, keep a clean camp.

WILDCATS

Cougar (*Felis concolor*) and bobcat (*Felis rufus*) inhabit the Pecos Wilderness. Neither is common and even coming across their tracks or other sign is rare. Each is solitary in habit. Chief prey of cougar is mule deer, while bobcat subsist largely on rabbits, rodents, and birds. Mating for both species occurs most commonly in March and April. Anywhere from one to six mountain lion kittens are born after a gestation of 82 to 96 days; one to seven bobcat kittens arrive following a pregnancy lasting about 70 days.

Both inhabit rocky country and forested mountains; they are not usually seen on tundra. Dens are commonly found in rocky areas, boulder fields, and beneath logs. Generally very shy of humans, the cougar is most active in the day while the bobcat is more active at night.

MARMOT (*Marmota flaviventris*)

This is the largest ground-dwelling rodent native to the Southwest and is closely related to the ground squirrel. The marmot is a large, cat-sized mammal inhabiting timberline areas. It can also be found in spruce-fir forest, meadows, rock slides, and above timberline. The marmot ranges from yellowish brown to grays to blackish in color and has a short, bushy tail. It is yellow underneath.

This critter lives in a burrow built in rock clefts, under boulders, or in coarse, rocky soil. It feeds on grasses and other green vegetation, putting on a good layer of fat for winter hibernation which begins in October. The marmot is an early riser and enjoys "catching rays" on a boulder in the morning. It emits a shrill chirp or whistle when alarmed and quickly disappears into its burrow. Predators include bear, mountain lion, and eagle.

The marmot lives alone, in pairs, or in harems of a male and several females and their young. Mating occurs in spring after hibernation. The female gives birth to a litter of four or five young which are ready to be on their own by the time of the next hibernation. It becomes easily accustomed to humans and is not afraid to beg or to bite the human hand that feeds it.

BEAVER (*Castor canadensis*)

The beaver is a member of the rodent family which also includes the rat, gopher, and squirrel. This semiaquatic animal weighs about 60 pounds, is over four feet long including the tail, and has dark brown fur. Its webbed hind feet, small ears, and large, flattened, scale-covered tail are adaptations to its environment.

The beaver lives in family groups along permanent, tree-covered creeks. It usually builds a dam of sticks, rocks, and mud to make a pond on the creek. Its dome-shaped, stick-and-mud lodge with an underwater entrance is built in these ponds but the beaver may also burrow into stream banks.

The beaver feeds on the bark and cambium layer of trees and shrubs, especially aspen, birch, and willow. It may dig canals from a good food source to its pond to facilitate transportation of the food. It is most active at night, but may be seen cruising in the pond in early evening. When disturbed, the beaver slaps its tail on the water surface, making a loud sound which is presumed to be a warning to other beavers. The beaver remains active in winter, living on food stored at the bottom of the pond.

Beaver ponds cause major ecological changes in the surrounding area. Flooding kills trees which then provide homes for cavity-nesting birds.

Water-loving plants which grow in the pond provide food and shelter for many animals. As the water table rises, it stimulates vegetative growth. The pond and surrounding wet areas prevent rapid storm runoff and ensure steady year-round stream flow for trout and other fish. When the pond silts in, it becomes covered with meadow grasses and becomes a rich food source for grazing animals.

TREE SQUIRRELS

The most common squirrel seen in the wilderness is the red squirrel (*Tamiasciurus hudsonicus*). This rodent lives in the spruce-fir forests of the Pecos. It is a small tree squirrel about 13 inches long and weighs about half a pound. The red squirrel has a prominent black stripe along each side of its body which is reddish above and white below. The tail is narrow and shorter than the body with a black edge and tip.

Abert's squirrel (*Sciurus aberti*) is much less common and may be found in the ponderosa pine areas of the wilderness. It is almost twice as large as the red squirrel, gray in color with white below. Each ear has a long, conspicuous tuft of hair which appears in autumn.

Squirrels are active throughout the year, feeding on leaf buds, flowers, herbs, mushrooms, acorns, and conifer seeds. They store spruce and fir cones in hollow logs or under piles of leaves. When needed, the cones are excavated and the seeds eaten. Piles of cone scales can get two to three feet deep. These middens also mark territory.

Tree squirrels make nests of plant material built on a branch near the trunk of a tree. Litters of three or four young are born in late spring or early summer. Squirrels fill the forest with their constant chattering and scolding.

GROUND SQUIRRELS

The rock (*Spermophilus variegatus*) and golden-mantled (*Spermophilus lateralis*) ground squirrels are other common inhabitants of the wilderness.

The rock squirrel is a large ground squirrel with a long bushy tail and mottled gray back. It can be mistaken for a tree squirrel, but a rock squirrel generally has shorter ears and a less bushy tail lacking white fringe. It averages 19 inches in length and weighs about 1 pound 11 ounces. It feeds on fruits, flowers, and seeds.

The golden-mantled ground squirrel is 11 inches long and weighs about seven ounces. Like other ground squirrels, it has facial stripes and the black stripe down the middle of the back. It has a white stripe running from shoulder to hip on each side of the back. The tail is white with gray and is yellowish below. It prefers meadow and forest edge environments and dwells in burrows. It feeds on mushrooms, leaves, flowers, and fruits. It begins hibernation in August and breeds in spring, the females giving birth to litters of two to seven young.

CHIPMUNKS

Least (*Eutamias minimus*) and Colorado (*Eutamius quadrivittatus*) chipmunks are the two chipmunks most likely to be seen in the Pecos, and are difficult to tell apart. The chipmunk has evenly spaced longitudinal stripes on the back, a long hairy tail, long pointed ears, and stripes on its face. The least chipmunk runs with its tail held up. This rodent is six to nine inches long and weighs about two ounces. It lives in an underground burrow under tree roots or in rocky terrain and stores food for winter. The chipmunk does not hibernate but may stay underground for up to three weeks during inclement or extremely cold weather.

PIKA (*Ochotona princeps*)

Also known as *coney*, the pika is found in or near rock slides on talus slopes from the spruce-fir zone to alpine tundra. Guinea pig–sized, it may be sighted on prominent rocks in the slides. You may also hear its distinctive call—a nasal bleat. In summer, it gathers and cures vegetation which will be found spread on rocks to dry in the sun. This hay is stored for later use. Active all year, the pika mates in summer. Within 30 days, two to six young are born. The weasel is a major predator of the pika.

SNOWSHOE HARE (*Lepus americanus*)

This hare is found mainly in spruce-fir forest with a dense understory of shrubs and small trees. It rests by day in small depressions in areas of dense cover. In autumn, the decreasing daylight causes production of white hairs. The summer brown is moulted and the now all-white hare is camouflaged in the snow. The snowshoe hare is an important food for many predators. It feeds on the various vegetative parts of plants, and also on the bark and cambium layer of trees. Its hind feet have a broad web of hair during winter which makes for easier walking and running over deep snows.

MOUNTAIN COTTONTAIL RABBIT (*Sylvilagus nuttalli*)

This species is found from ponderosa pine forest to higher elevations. Usually most active at dawn and dusk, it also feeds at night on leaves, stems, flowers, roots, and bark. The cottontail favors areas where high-quality cover (thick brush, rock, old burrows) is close when danger threatens. Courtship consists of the male chasing the female and urinating on her. The female may produce three or four litters a year. Like the larger snowshoe hare, the cottontail is an important food for many predators.

BIRDS

WHITE-TAILED PTARMIGAN (*Lagopus leucurus*)

The white-tailed ptarmigan, also called snow grouse, inhabits subalpine zones from northern New Mexico to south-central Alaska. This bird is 12 to 13 inches long. The summer plumage is brown with a white belly, wings, and tail; in winter it is pure white except for black eyes and bill.

In New Mexico, it historically occurred in scattered locations of the Sangre de Cristo Mountains. It was extremely rare and was completely extirpated from much of its northern New Mexico range, including the Pecos Wilderness. Confirmed sightings of ptarmigan in New Mexico were lacking from the early 1900s until the late 1970s, when there were a few in the Wheeler Peak, Latir Peak, and Costilla Peak areas. During the summer of 1981 the Forest Service and the New Mexico Game and Fish Department reintroduced ptarmigan into the Pecos Wilderness. Now it is commonly seen along the Santa Barbara Divide.

Suitable summer habitat for the nesting bird is the alpine tundra. The nest is a shallow depression lined with fine grass, lichens, and small leaves, usually on exposed alpine turf, under shrubs, on steep slopes, or between rocks above timberline. During summer, leaves, flowers, buds, seeds, and bulbs of sedges and herbaceous broad-leaved plants are important food for adults. Chicks feed on both insects and vegetation.

TURKEY (*Meleagris gallopavo*)

In the Pecos Wilderness the wild turkey is associated with ponderosa pine and mixed conifer habitats in areas with snags or open-topped trees which are used for roosting. It forages mostly on the ground and important food sources include grasses, seeds, and acorns. In winter when there is typically lots of snow on the ground, it feeds on the buds of trees and may go up to a week at a time without food. In early spring, it depends on fresh green grass and buds. During summer, insects, especially grasshoppers, are eaten regularly. It will also eat fruits, leaves of plants, and some frogs, lizards, and snakes.

In late winter the so-called gobbling season begins. The gobbler (male turkey) defends a territory and drives rivals away from the hens he attracts. Harems of about five or six females are gathered. Nesting sites are close to a water source and normally well concealed by low vegetation. Eggs are laid between February and July and the incubation period lasts about 28 days. The female alone is responsible for incubation. After hatching, the young soon begin feeding on their own and within a week the chicks are making short flights and roosting in trees, where they are less vulnerable to predation. Sometimes two or more hens with broods join company and family groups stay together until the next breeding season. The males usually remain in separate small flocks until the next gobbling season.

BLUE GROUSE (*Dendragapus obscurus*)

The blue grouse, also called the dusky or sooty grouse, is found mainly in spruce-fir, mixed conifer, and aspen forests of the Pecos Wilderness. In winter, it inhabits the conifer forests where its main foods are needles, buds, twigs, and seeds from fir trees. As winter ends, the blue grouse moves to lower altitudes into aspen groves and forest edge habitats.

In early spring, the male begins establishing hooting territories in areas with a combination of fairly heavy cover for escape and relatively open areas for display. The male uses a series of low-pitched, owl-like calls to proclaim its territory. Most hooting occurs in the early morning and again in the evening and serves to attract females. The presence of females produces intense strutting displays by the males.

The hen generally nests in a habitat that provides opportunities for the young to forage for insects. Typical nesting sites are under old logs or among the roots of fallen trees in fairly open timber. Adults feed mainly on plant material, nearly two-thirds of it being conifer needles, the rest being flowers, fruits, and a few insects. Eggs are laid from April through August with an incubation period of 26 days. After hatching the chicks become self-sufficient very quickly. The broods initially use largely grasses and non-woody weeds as cover. As these open habitats dry out, the birds move into aspen thickets. Gradually, broods break up and the young disperse singly or in small groups, slowly working their way upward toward the wintering range.

STELLER'S JAY (*Cyanocitta stelleri*)

Common throughout the ponderosa pine, mixed conifer, and spruce-fir habitats, this bird is bold and well known around picnic grounds and campsites, but shy in open woods and difficult to approach. It ranges up to the 11,000-foot elevations and sometimes travels in flocks of a dozen or more. It forages both in treetops and on the ground, typically eating nuts, seeds, fruits, insects, frogs, eggs, and small birds. In winter, Steller's jay migrates from the mountains down to the lowlands.

Steller's jay is a large bird—12 to 13 inches long—and is the only western jay with a crest. The foreparts and beak are black; the rear parts (wings, tail, belly) are dark blue. It builds its twiggy, root-lined nest in conifers.

GRAY JAY (*Perisoreus canadensis*)

This is a large gray bird, smoke gray above, lighter gray below, with white on the forehead and throat. It favors coniferous forests, wintering throughout its breeding range with altitudinal migration to lower elevations in late fall through winter. The gray jay's natural diet is primarily insects, fruits, and carrion. It is very tame, bold, and curious, showing no fear of humans and brazenly raiding camps and picnic tables.

CLARK'S NUTCRACKER (*Nucifraga columbiana*)

This bird is sometimes mistaken for the gray jay. Both are found in the same habitats—ponderosa pine, mixed conifer, and spruce-fir forests. Clark's nutcracker has an even gray body with conspicuous white patches on its black wings and tail. It often breeds early at high elevations while snow is still deep on the ground. During late summer and fall it caches conifer seeds which provide its major food source from winter to mid-summer. The caches are believed to be found by memory. In summer it hops or walks on the ground, foraging for insects, grubs, nuts, snails, and carrion. It also sometimes eats eggs and young small birds.

Like the gray jay, Clark's nutcracker is noisy, boisterous, and extremely curious. It follows coyotes or passing deer, comes readily to imitations of owls, and comes around camps for food scraps.

RAVEN (*Corvus corax*)

This bird is often mistaken for the common crow. The raven is larger (21 to 27 inches) and has a heavier, thicker-looking bill than the crow. This all-black bird has a wedge-shaped tail and shaggy throat feathers. When flying, it alternates flapping with soaring, similar to hawks; it soars on flat wings while the crow soars with wings bent upward. The raven is found in all areas of the wilderness. Its nest is a mass of sticks and bones usually located on cliffs but sometimes in trees. The raven eats a variety of foods including carrion, seeds, fruits, and insects. It has a loud, hoarse, croaking call and also a hollow knocking call.

RAPTORS

Raptors are the birds of prey such as hawks, eagles, falcons, owls, and vultures. These birds include several of the most beautiful and impressive creatures on earth. All raptors except vultures catch their food. Aside from owls, which hunt at night, almost all other raptors are daytime hunters.

Some, like the falcons, hunt at high speeds. The accipiters, which include the sharp-shinned hawk, goshawk, and Cooper's hawk, have great maneuverability. When hunting, the accipiter darts low and swift through the forest and may snatch a bird out of the air or surprise and strike one on the ground or a perch. Others, like the red-tailed hawk and eagles, soar high in the sky, watching the ground for mice, ground squirrels, rabbits, and other prey. But most hunting by raptors is done from perches where they can scan the surrounding terrain with their binocular-like vision, possibly the keenest of any animal.

The Pecos is home to a wide variety of raptors. The golden eagle, red-tailed hawk, turkey vulture, and great horned owl are the most commonly seen raptors in the wilderness.

The golden eagle likes open habitats such as meadows and alpine tundra and usually feeds on rabbits, marmot, ground squirrels, and sometimes grouse and ptarmigan. Most nest in cliffs, some in conifers or on earthen mounds. Some pairs use the same nest year after year.

OTHER BIRDS

Hundreds of other species of birds such as hummingbirds, woodpeckers, flycatchers, bluebirds, warblers, finches, and sparrows also inhabit the Pecos Wilderness. The list is too numerous to discuss in detail. The Pecos/Las Vegas Ranger District Bird List (with associated habitat types) is available at the district office.

F I S H

Cutthroat, rainbow, and German brown are the three species of trout that thrive in the high-country lakes and streams of the Pecos Wilderness. Of the three, the cutthroat is the only native; the other two are introduced species.

Generally speaking, the farther into the wilderness you are, the better the fishing will be. The crystal-clear water of the lakes and beaver ponds will test even the most skillful angler. Along the streams, open stretches alternate with brush, overgrown sections and deep pools. Fishing is usually unproductive during the spring runoff but once the snowmelt has slowed it becomes excellent and stays that way.

Anybody over 12 years of age who is fishing must possess a valid New Mexico fishing license available from the New Mexico Department of Game and Fish or from local vendors. Information on regulations, fees, bag limits, and other matters is available from the department; write to New Mexico Department of Game and Fish, Villagra Building, Santa Fe, NM 87503, or call 505/827-7911.

SUGGESTED READING

SUGGESTED READING

A thorough bibliography of the Pecos Wilderness and northern New Mexico would fill many pages. The following list of books is admittedly incomplete but nonetheless useful for those who wish to learn more about the history and natural history of the Pecos Wilderness.

HISTORY

Ancient Ruins of the Southwest by David Grant Noble; Northland Press, 1989

A guidebook to western archaeological ruins. Illustrated with black-and-white photographs.

I Am Here: Two Thousand Years of Southwest Indian Arts and Culture by Andrew Hunter Whiteford et al.; Museum of New Mexico Press, 1989

Essays by noted scholars discuss the change and continuity of Indian culture and craft work over a period of two thousand years. Beautifully illustrated with color and black-and-white photographs.

Beatty's Cabin by Elliott S. Barker; Calvin Horn, 1988

Adventures in the Pecos high country by one who knew it best.

New Mexico: An Interpretive History by Marc Simmons; University of New Mexico Press, 1988

Simmons writes with knowledge and sensitivity of the diverse cultures that make up the social fabric of New Mexico; possibly the best short history of the state.

Enchantment and Exploitation: The Life and Hard Times of a New Mexico Mountain Range by William deBuys; University of New Mexico Press, 1985

Ecological and cultural history of the Sangre de Cristo Mountains.

River of Traps by William deBuys and Alex Harris; University of New Mexico Press, 1990

Life in Las Trampas, a small New Mexico village on the fringes of the Pecos Wilderness. "A beautiful book about water, people, land. . . ."

Roadside History of New Mexico by Francis L. and Roberta B. Fugate; Mountain Press, 1989

This book gives readers an appreciation of the past as they travel in the present . . . and a deeper insight into the rich history of New Mexico.

NATURAL HISTORY

Soft Paths by Bruce Hampton and David Cole; Stackpole Books, 1988

Unquestionably the best book on "no-impact" camping. Techniques developed at the National Outdoor Leadership School, where Hampton is a senior staff instructor, lessen the impact campers and wilderness travelers make on the land.

Winter: An Ecological Handbook by James C. Halfpenny and R. D. Ozanne; Johnson Books, 1990

Everything (and more) anybody ever needed to know about winter; from the stress of cold on animals, plants, and people, to adaptations to extreme winter conditions, and advice on winter camping techniques and equipment.

GUIDES AND FIELD GUIDES—PLANTS

Alpine Wildflowers of the Rocky Mountains by Joseph F. Duft and Robert K. Moseley; Mountain Press, 1989

A guide to the flowers of the alpine zone along the Rocky Mountain crest from the Canadian Rockies to northern New Mexico.

The Audubon Society Nature Guides: Western Forests by Stephen Whitney; Alfred A. Knopf, 1985

A comprehensive field guide, fully illustrated with color photographs, to the trees, wildflowers, birds, reptiles, insects, and other natural wonders of North America's forests.

Edible Wild Plants of the Rocky Mountains by H. D. Harrington; University of New Mexico Press, 1967

A useful guide to the edible native vegetation. Illustrated.

Flowering Plants of New Mexico by Robert DeWitt Ivy; published by the author, 1986

One of the most comprehensive guides to the plants of New Mexico.

Medicinal Plants of the Mountain West by Michael Moore; Museum of New Mexico Press, 1979

A study of the medicinal herbs; their uses, methods of collecting, and preparations. Index of Latin, English, and Spanish names.

100 Roadside Wildflowers of the Southwest Woodlands by Janice E. Bowers; Southwest Parks and Monuments Association, 1987

Revised and updated with color photographs of interesting southwestern wildflowers.

GUIDES AND FIELD GUIDES—BIRDS

National Geographic Society's Field Guide to the Birds of North America by John L. Dunn et al.; 1983

Considered by many to be the best book on North American birds.

Peterson Field Guide to Western Birds by Roger Tory Peterson; Houghton Mifflin, 1990

The new, third edition of Peterson's *Western Birds*. New color paintings of all the birds west of the Great Plains, new color maps, and a completely revised and updated text.

Peterson Field Guide to Hawks by William S. Clark and Brian K. Wheeler; Houghton Mifflin, 1988

A field guide devoted exclusively to raptors.

GUIDES AND FIELD GUIDES—MAMMALS

America's Great Cats by Gary Turbak; Northland Press, 1986

Brief chapters on each of the wild felines of North America. With color photographs.

A Field Guide to Mammal Tracking by James Halfpenny; Johnson Books, 1986

Possibly the best book available on the subject, it brings the amateur naturalist the latest information on animal gaits and scat.

Peterson Field Guide to Mammals by William H. Burt and Richard P. Grossendeider; Houghton Mifflin, 1987

One of the distinguished Peterson field guide series, *Mammals* has long been the standard reference work for field identification.

The Natural History of New Mexican Mammals by James S. Findley; University of New Mexico Press, 1987

Identifies and describes 149 species of mammals found in New Mexico. 33 color plates.

Twilight Hunters by Gary Turbak; Northland Press, 1987

A beautifully photographed book on the wild canines of North America.

GUIDES AND FIELD GUIDES—GEOLOGY

Geology of the Upper Pecos by Patrick K. Southerland and Arthur Montgomery; New Mexico Institute of Technology, 1990

New edition of the earlier work, this book is also a trail guide.

Geologic Map of New Mexico by the Geologic Society of New Mexico

Underground New Mexico: the formations that make up the state.

Roadside Geology of New Mexico by Halka Chronic; Mountain Press, 1988

One in a series of books on geology based on a road-by-road study of the structure of the earth as revealed from a car window.

GUIDES AND FIELD GUIDES—MISCELLANEOUS

Golden Field Guide to Reptiles by Hobart M. Smith and Edmund D. Brodie Jr.; Golden Press, 1982

One of the Golden Field Guide series, this is a useful guide for field identification.

Ninety-nine Gnats, Nits, and Nibblers by May R. Berenbaum; University of Illinois Press, 1989

A delightful armchair guide to the lives of some of the more common insects. Informative, humorous, and scientifically accurate.

Peterson First Guide to Astronomy by Jay M. Pasachoff; Houghton Mifflin, 1988

An easy-to-read introduction to the subject.

The Weather Companion by Gary Lockhart; John Wiley & Sons Inc., 1988

Stories, anecdotes, and lots of useful information about all kinds of weather phenomena; an album of meteorological history, science, legend, and folklore.

TRAVEL

Journey to the High Southwest by Robert L. Cagey; Globe Pequot Press, 1988

An excellent guide to the Four Corners region in Arizona, Colorado, New Mexico, and Utah. Things to do, sights to see, places to stay.

New Mexico Traveler's Handbook by Bill Weir; Moon Publications, 1988

A well-researched guide with information on places to go, motel, restaurant and campground listings, trail maps, history, travel, and recreation.

Scenic Byways by Beverly Magley; Falcon Press, 1990

A guide to some of the most beautiful roads in America—the scenic byways of our national forests.